What the Critics said of Kavaljit Singh's previous book

TAMING GLOBAL FINANCIAL FLOWS

"Kavaljit Singh has made a difficult subject intelligible to ordinary citizens, and in a very readable way he has mapped out the progressive alternatives for bringing international finance under democratic control."
Edward S. Herman

"We can always count on Kavaljit Singh for lucid and hard-hitting analysis. This book is no exception."
Susan George

"Singh is to be congratulated... an up-to-date critical assessment of financial globalization."
David Felix

"Taming Global Financial Flows is a thought-provoking book...It aims at an encyclopedic reach in terms of ideas and comments on almost every aspect of this fascinating subject."
S. Venkitaramanan

"Kavaljit's book outlines with impressive clarity extremely complex and crucial issues... A must for all students of international finance as well as for policy makers and interested NGOs."
Stephany Griffith-Jones

"... Should be made compulsory reading for all finance ministers, central bankers, economic policy makers... learned international experts."
Arun Ghosh

"An indispensable guide to the turbulent world of finance."
Third World Resurgence

"Kavaljit Singh may not be the new Keynes, but, his new book provides a detailed and clear exposition of many elements in the puzzle. There is useful material for activists and citizens' groups to consider, if they want to engage with the realities of power."
The Ecologist

"Well-known globalization gadfly and critic Kavaljit Singh has compiled a simple-to-read yet in-depth study of the tumultuous global financial system."
Resource Center of the Americas

Contents

List of Boxes

List of Tables

Acronyms

ADB	Asian Development Bank
APEC	Asia-Pacific Economic Cooperation
BIS	Bank for International Settlements
BoP	balance of payments
CAL	capital account liberalization
CEE	Central and Eastern Europe
EMH	efficient market hypothesis
ERM	Exchange Rate Mechanism
EU	European Union
FDI	foreign direct investment
FSA	Financial Services Agreement
GATT	General Agreement on Tariffs and Trade
GATS	General Agreement on Trade in Services
GDP	gross domestic product
G-7	group of seven highly industrialized countries
G-20	group of twenty developing countries
HIPCs	heavily indebted poor countries
IADB	Inter-American Development Bank
ICSID	International Centre for Settlement on Investment Disputes
IFI	international financial institution
IMF	International Monetary Fund
MAI	Multilateral Agreement on Investment
MERCOSUR	Southern Common Market
MFN	most favored nation
MIGA	Multilateral Investment Guarantee Agency

M&A	merger and acquisition
NAFTA	North American Free Trade Agreement
NATO	North Atlantic Treaty Organization
NED	National Endowment for Democracy
NEPAD	New Partnership for Africa's Development
NGO	non-governmental organization
NIEO	new international economic order
NT	national treatment
OECD	Organization of Economic Cooperation and Development
PRSP	poverty reduction strategy paper
R&D	research and development
SDR	special drawing right
SME	small and medium-sized enterprise
SOE	state-owned enterprise
TRIMs	trade-related investment measures
TRIPs	trade-related aspects of intellectual property rights
TNC	transnational corporation
UK	United Kingdom
UN	United Nations
UNCTAD	United Nations Conference on Trade and Development
UNDP	United Nations Development Programme
UNICEF	United Nations Children's Fund
US	United States of America
WTO	World Trade Organization

Data Notes

Million is 1000000.

Billion is 1000 million.

Trillion is 1000 billion.

Dollars are US dollars unless otherwise specified.

Acknowledgments and Dedication

I am indebted to all those people who helped in the preparation and final publication of this book. Since a very large number of individuals and institutions have helped in the preparation of the book in one way or the other, it is not feasible to acknowledge their names. In particular, I would like to thank my colleagues at Asia-Europe Dialogue Project, Asia Pacific Research Network, Biswajit Dhar, Reality of Aid Network and Tony Tujan for providing intellectual and institutional support. Thanks are also due to all those whose writings and data I have drawn upon in the preparation of the book. The library staff of American Centre, British Council and United Nations Information Centre provided excellent support in terms of research papers, books, journals and newspapers. Special thanks are due to Dilip Upadhyaya and Shivani Sood for their help in editing of the manuscript. As usual, Ranjeet Thakur provided excellent computer and secretarial support. I am also deeply indebted to Robert Molteno of Zed Books for his encouragement and patience. My sincere apologies to all those who have been inadvertently left out. Errors, of course, are mine alone.

Finally, I owe a special debt to Fabby, Ishu and my mother for their enormous support, and to whom this book is dedicated.

Introduction

> The ideas of economists and political philosophers, both when they are right and when they are wrong, are more powerful than is commonly understood. Indeed, the world is ruled by little else. Practical men, who believe themselves to be quite exempt from any intellectual influences, are usually the slave of some defunct economist.
>
> *John Maynard Keynes*

Globalization has become the cliché of our times. Though the term globalization is widely used, it is not amenable to precise definition. Evolving a common understanding of globalization is an uphill task because the term connotes different things to different people. Broadly speaking, globalization refers to intensification of trans-border interconnectedness in all spheres of economy, politics, society and culture. In other words, globalization refers to a world in which complex economic, political, social and cultural processes operate and interact without any influence of national boundaries and distance. It also implies that a development in any part of the world can create far-reaching consequences elsewhere.

In academic literature, several terms such as 'Globality,' 'Globaloney,' 'Internationalization,' 'Universalization,' 'Westernization,' 'Americanization,' 'Transnationalization,' and 'Deterritorialization' have been used to characterize the intensification of trans-border linkages in the spheres of economy, politics, culture and society. Without further elaborating the precise definition of these terms, it needs to be emphasized that there are substantial distinctions between them.

More often than not, analysts conceive the process of globalization predominantly in economic terms with no linkages to politics, history, culture, environment and society. This may be off the mark since globalization encompasses several non-economic processes. Since this book is primarily concerned with the economic globalization, other important components of globalization have not been addressed. Economic globalization — though not only an economic phenomenon — essentially refers to breaking down of national barriers on trade, production and finance. The cross-border movement of trade and capital flows is often used as an indicator of economic globalization.

Any analysis of globalization would remain incomplete without situating it in the wider context of capitalism, which is facing a deep systemic crisis since the early 1970s. The contemporary economic globalization consisting of two distinct features — the globalization of production (related to trade, production and real economy) and the globalization of finance — gained momentum after the collapse of Bretton Woods system in the early seventies. The regime was strengthened by the widespread acceptance of neoliberal orthodoxy based on fiscal prudence, deregulation, privatization and liberalization, known in popular parlance as 'Washington Consensus.' With technological advances in the communication and information technology, there has been rapid expansion of trade and private capital flows across borders.

Contrary to neoliberal presumptions, the contemporary globalization is neither a natural nor an autonomous phenomenon. Rather it has been shaped by complex and dynamic set of interactions between transnational capital and nation-states.

For the transnational elites, corporations and fund managers, globalization offers new opportunities to penetrate world markets as countries are eliminating barriers on trade and capital flows. While on the other hand, labor and popular movements are becoming increasingly apprehensive about the negative fallout of globalization on the livelihoods of poor people. For most people irrespective of their location, the benefits offered by globalization of trade and capital flows are yet to be materialized. Instead, the era of global economic integration has witnessed sluggish economic growth, worsening of the living conditions, occurrence of financial crises and greater social and political conflicts. The policies associated with globalization have also contributed in the deterioration of education, health and other social indicators in many parts of the world.

Growing income inequality, both within and between countries, has been a characteristic feature of contemporary globalization. Globalization, in fact, is an inherently uneven process which has a tendency to further accentuate inequality both within and among countries by pampering certain classes and regions over others. The asymmetry is best reflected in the globalization of financial markets where owners and managers of financial capital move trillions of dollars every day through computerized dealing systems while labor mobility is getting severely constricted, except in the case of highly skilled professionals whose number, in any case, is minuscule. The paradox of globalization is that it unifies and integrates the rich and affluent classes while marginalizing the poor masses who lack requisite skills and resources to profit from world markets.

The growing public anxiety and backlash against globalization is becoming apparent day by day. From right-wing politicians in the North to left-wing popular movements in the South, the backlash against globalization has taken global contours. The chasm between the hyper-globalists and anti-globalists is far from bridged. As the positions on both sides of the divide harden, the debate on globalization is getting further confounded. The globalization debate is still on and there are no signs of it getting resolved in the near future.

The idea of this book originated during an informal conversation with political activists and researchers gathered at an international conference on globalization in Bangkok in early 2002. Many of them expressed the need for a non-technical exposé on the contemporary debates related to globalization. Although a number of books are nowadays available on globalization issues, yet very few focus on major contemporary debates. One is not denying the existence of voluminous literature on contemporary debates but much of it is available in a highly technical language essentially addressed to academic and policy circles. The publication of such materials in highly specialized academic journals makes it inaccessible to activists, students and general public. The book is intended to fill this lacuna.

The main purpose was not to write a lengthy academic text but a non-technical, popular book which could be easily comprehended by students, activists and concerned citizens. Instead of focusing on past debates related to globalization, the book makes a critical analysis of the contemporary issues. Written for a non-technical audience and lay readership, the book sheds light on the ongoing debates while dispelling several myths associated with the globalization processes. It critically examines the viewpoints held by both the hyper-globalists and zealous anti-globalists.

The book does not deal with all major contemporary debates on globalization. I have deliberately chosen only those contemporary issues that require in-depth analysis and study in view of their profound implications on economy, society and politics. Unlike usual academic books, the book has been formatted in such a manner to ensure that different chapters can be read on their own. The book is organized into five chapters. Chapter 1 addresses issues related to contemporary financial liberalization and globalization. It particularly deals with questions such as whether free movement of finance capital across borders really promotes economic growth and development? Looking at the experience of several countries that have adopted financial liberalization, the chapter examines the exponential rise of finance capital and its wider consequences on growth and development on a world scale. Besides, issues related to the role of volatile finance capital in perpetuating different types of financial crises have been dealt with. The chapter debunks several popular myths associated with the benefits of financial globalization. The wider developmental implications of market driven banking industry are delineated in details. The chapter also provides a critical commentary on the global marketing of microfinance as a panacea for poverty alleviation.

Chapter 2 examines the rationale and wider consequences of global investment rules. At present, there is no comprehensive multilateral agreement on foreign investment. With the collapse of negotiations on MAI at the OECD in the late 1990s, renewed efforts have been made to establish global investment rules at the WTO. Notwithstanding the collapse of WTO Ministerial Conference in Cancun, developed countries have been employing myriad strategies to force consensus on investment issues. But many developing countries have been adamant to stop negotiations on investment issues at the WTO since it has the potential to cause them serious economic damage. This chapter critically examines the history of investment rules, present status of negotiations, and recent experiences with bilateral and regional investment agreements. The chapter also dispels several popular myths associated with the benefits of multilateral investment agreement in the light of empirical evidence.

There is a strong tendency among many political analysts to interpret globalization and democracy as compatible and complementary phenomena. But, in reality, globalization and democracy involve several complex and paradoxical processes that enmesh unevenly at various levels. Chapter 3 deals with such issues. As is well known, democracy encompasses a much wider canvas than being a mere instrument for facilitating the expansion of market economy at the global level. It explains that democracy cannot be attained through privatization, deregulation and movement of goods and capital across borders. Nor could it be attained by the availability of jeans, colas, burgers, pop music and computers. This chapter scrutinizes all such relevant issues including 'globalization of democracy' from a critical perspective. Issues such as delinking of economic decision-making from democratic political processes and the ascendancy of technocratic forms of governance are also examined. The chapter strongly underscores the viewpoint that genuine democracy is not viable without a radical restructuring of contemporary globalization.

Chapter 4 critically appraises the emergence of 'good governance' agenda in the international development aid. The earlier policy agenda of 'getting prices right' has been replaced by 'getting institutions right.' Pushed by powerful international financial institutions, 'good governance' has become the cornerstone of international development cooperation. Nowadays it would be difficult to find aid or loan packages of multilateral financial institutions and bilateral donors that do not contain governance conditionalities. The chapter examines the discernible shift in the policies of international aid community, particularly of the international financial institutions, towards good governance both as an objective and a precondition for development aid. By negating the issues of politics, power relations and interest groups, the aid agencies have solely relied on the technocratic approaches towards governance issues. Their resistance to admit that governance issues are political issues stems from their false notion of 'political neutrality' and their ideological moorings which delinks economic issues from politics. The chapter stresses the need to move away from the superficial boundaries of 'technocratic consensus' and start addressing governance issues as political issues.

Chapter 5 seeks answers to the pertinent question: Does omnipotent markets mean impotent politicians? Many commentators have equated the ascendancy of globalization as the demise of nation-states.

Dramatic catchphrases such as 'The End of Nation-State,' 'The Retreat of the State' and 'The End of Sovereignty' are commonly used to explain such viewpoints. Nevertheless, such simplistic viewpoints fail to capture the essence of the complex relationship between globalization and nation-states. There is no denying that growing domination exercised by transnational capital poses new challenges to the national authorities for pursuing independent economic policies but it would be off the mark to conclude that nation-state is going to wither away or become irrelevant.

With the help of real world examples, this chapter negates the notion that states have become insignificant in the present age of globalization. It highlights the growing role and importance of certain powerful states in shaping the contours of contemporary globalization. This chapter argues that as a legitimate source of governance, the role of state in global governance will remain quintessential in the future. The chapter contends that the discourse should move beyond the rhetoric that all state interventions are evil and all markets are sacrosanct. Rather the focus should be on what kind of strategies, policies and regulations are required to make both markets and states accountable and democratic in order to strengthen economic, social and political rights of the citizens. By challenging the notions that globalization is an irreversible phenomenon and 'there is no alternative,' the chapter affirms that political processes can reverse the march towards globalization.

CHAPTER 1

Does Financial Globalization Stimulate Investment and Growth?

> Speculators would do no harm as bubbles on a steady stream of
> enterprise. But the position is serious when enterprise becomes
> the bubble in the whirlpool of speculation. When the capital
> development of a country becomes a by-product of the activities
> of a casino, the job is likely to be ill-done.
>
> *John Maynard Keynes*

TILL recently, the conventional wisdom among policymakers was
that free flow of capital across borders brings in enormous benefits
for both the source and the recipient countries. The proponents of
financial globalization have long argued that freeing the financial
sector from government intervention and allowing the free flow of
capital across borders would lead to increased availability of investment, efficient allocation of savings into more productive use on
global scale, higher economic growth, diversification of risky assets
and healthy discipline for governments that encourage better economic policies. The stated benefits of financial liberalization include higher savings, enhancement of efficiency of financial inter-
mediation by removing 'distortions' created by controls, greater
competition in financial markets and improvement in monetary
control. The arguments in favor of financial globalization are largely
based on an analogy between goods and financial markets, overlooking the simple fact that financial markets are prone to asymmetric information, herd behavior, moral hazard and self-fulfilling

prophecies. Liberalization of capital account has been proclaimed as the quintessential measure for countries to benefit from global capital mobility. As noted by Stanley Fischer, former Deputy Managing Director of the International Monetary Fund (IMF):

> Put abstractly, free capital movements facilitate a more efficient global allocation of saving and help channel resources into their most productive uses, thus increasing economic growth and welfare. From the individual country's perspective, the benefits take the form of increases in both the potential pool of investible funds and the access of domestic residents to foreign capital markets. From the viewpoint of the international economy, open capital accounts support the multilateral trading system by broadening the channels through which developed and developing countries alike can finance trade and investment and attain higher levels of income.[1]

Based on the efficient markets hypothesis (EMH), the neoliberal thinking on financial globalization — consisting of two mutually reinforcing processes, namely, financial liberalization and capital account liberalization — held sway in both theory and practice since the early 1970s. Within a few years of its enunciation, the EMH gained strong foothold in academic and policy circles. The University of Chicago became the nerve center of finance theory and practice. Under its influence, countries started liberalizing their domestic financial sector and removing restrictions on the movement of capital across borders. Majority of developed countries had achieved considerable financial liberalization and globalization by the end of the 1970s while the developing countries initiated these processes in the 1980s and 1990s.

It needs to be emphasized here that financial reforms in developing countries were not introduced as isolated policy measures but were important components of the Washington

Consensus. In particular, the IMF has been aggressively promoting financial liberalization and capital account liberalization in the borrowing countries. IMF is not the only multilateral financial institution promoting financial liberalization. Its twin, the World Bank had also encouraged financial liberalization in the past. However, in the wake of the Southeast Asian financial crisis, the Bank has done some rethinking on its previous position while the IMF continues to prescribe liberalization of capital account. Obligations

---

Box 1.1

Financial Liberalization and Capital Account Liberalization

Financial liberalization is a process in which allocation of resources is determined by market forces. It minimizes the role of the state in the financial sector by encouraging market forces to decide who gets and gives credit and at what price. The key components of financial liberalization include deregulation of interest rates; removal of credit controls; privatization of government owned banks and financial institutions; liberalization of restrictions on the entry of private sector and/ or foreign banks and financial institutions into domestic financial markets; and introduction of market-based instruments of monetary control.

Capital account liberalization (CAL) is the process through which countries liberalize their capital account by removing controls, taxes, subsidies and quantitative restrictions that affect capital account transactions. Capital account restrictions may include limiting domestic banks' foreign borrowing; limiting the entry of foreign capital; and restricting the repatriation of funds from the country. CAL entails dismantling of all barriers on international financial transactions and the purchase and sale of financial or real assets across borders. With full CAL, companies and individuals (both residents and non-residents) can move their financial resources and assets from country to country without any restrictions.

related to the liberalization of international capital transfers are also included in several regional treaties such as the North American Free Trade Agreement (NAFTA) and in Treaties of Friendship, Commerce and Navigation (FCN Treaties). In addition, financial liberalization has been institutionalized through various multilateral and regional agreements. In the case of the developed countries, Code of Liberalization of Capital Movements of the Organization of Economic Cooperation and Development (OECD) and the European Union (EU) Directives facilitated financial globalization.

Popular Myths about the Benefits of Financial Globalization

In the light of recent experiences, the notion that free flow of capital across borders offers immense benefits requires closer scrutiny. When capital flows freely across borders, do countries reap the benefits of increased investment? The answer is simply no. There is no evidence to prove conclusively that financial globalization leads to increased foreign investment in all countries. Nor does it boost the prospects of obtaining investment in future. Evidence collated from several developing countries has failed to establish any causal relationship between financial globalization and increased foreign investment. Since the 1980s, a large number of developing countries have carried out financial liberalization and capital account liberalization but only a handful of countries are receiving private capital flows. In an era of declining official aid and growing 'donor fatigue,' bulk of foreign direct investment (FDI) and portfolio flows have gone to a few developing countries such as China, Brazil, Mexico and Argentina in the 1990s. Only 14 countries account for over 85 per cent of private flows to the developing countries. While nearly 140 developing countries account for a mere 15 per cent of the FDI and 6 per cent of portfolio investment. This demonstrates that there is no positive correlation between capital account liberalization and increased investment.

A closer look at several African countries confirms that financial globalization does not guarantee increased investment. Since the early 1980s, many African countries have opened up their capital account and carried out comprehensive financial reforms but are receiving only a fraction of the global private capital flows. It is noteworthy that share of Africa in the FDI flows to the developing economies declined from 9 per cent in 1981-85 to just about 4 per cent in 1996-97. During the period 1990-96, Sub-Saharan Africa (excluding South Africa) received negligible net portfolio flows, while FDI flows (mostly related to exploitation of natural resources) were concentrated in a few countries such as Nigeria, Botswana, Ghana, Mozambique and Uganda. It is not lack of capital account liberalization and financial liberalization that prevents the flow of foreign investment to Africa, rather small size of domestic markets, poor infrastructure, locational disadvantages, civil unrest and political instability in the continent which are responsible for meager inflows. Essentially, capital tends to flow to countries where it is assured of higher returns and safety.

Latin America, no doubt, witnessed a surge in capital inflows in the 1990s. In Chile, Argentina, Brazil and Mexico, capital inflows were in the range of 5 to 10 per cent of the gross domestic product (GDP). But this unprecedented surge was not due to financial globalization since these countries had opened up their capital account much earlier as part of structural adjustment programs. Rather, a sharp decline in US interest rates coupled with the sudden attraction for 'emerging markets' by institutional investors fueled the surge in capital inflows in these countries.

Several countries (for instance, China, Taiwan and India) have been receiving substantial foreign investment with limited financial globalization. After the US, China has remained the top recipient of foreign investment in the 1990s. Every year, China attracts over $50 billion worth of foreign investment, bulk of it in the form of FDI. Malaysia, which re-imposed controls on its capital account in 1998, is receiving substantial amounts of FDI. These examples indicate that increased investment is neither automatic nor a necessary outcome of financial globalization.

Further, financial globalization can induce capital flight by legalizing capital outflows. In a financially liberalized regime, domestic capital can legally move out of the country to seek higher returns abroad. Capital flight has remained a persistent phenomenon afflicting many Latin American countries since the 1980s. To a large extent, international financial integration has further strengthened the process of capital flight from Africa. According to the World Bank, Africa — where capital is most scarce — had about 40 per cent of its private wealth held outside the continent.[2] In Sub-Saharan Africa, where profit remittances exceed net inflows of FDI since 1984, an estimated net transfer of $20 billion in the 1990s was recorded.

Another widespread notion persists in the corridors of financial markets and institutions that free movement of capital is vital for higher economic growth. There is little evidence linking financial globalization to growth. Financial openness by itself cannot enhance growth because it is a complex process, subject to a wide range of factors. If one tries to match the periods of financial globalization with the economic performance of countries, the results are contradictory. Growth started deteriorating around the 1970s when many countries moved towards capital account liberalization. The 1980s and the 1990s witnessed sharp deterioration in economic performance of many countries, both developed and the developing ones. The worst decadal-growth performance occurred in the 1990s. According to the IMF's *World Economic Outlook* (1999), average annual world output growth in the 1990s is now estimated at only 3.1 per cent, which is far below the average growth rates in the 1970s (4.4 per cent). In the developed countries, GDP growth in the 1980s and the 1990s was much lower than compared to the 1950s and the 1960s, described as the 'Golden Age' of capitalism. In the post-liberalization period, the average rate of growth has also witnessed a secular decline throughout the developing world.

The ratio of investment to GDP has remained lower in countries which embraced financial globalization. John Eatwell, while examining the changes in the share of investment to GDP in 54 countries between the Bretton Woods era of fixed exchange and capital controls (1960-71) and the current regime of open capital account found that the predominant tendency has been for investment to fall as a share of GDP.[3] "The decline is more pronounced in the period 1982-91 as capital liberalization has become more widespread, with two-thirds of the countries in the sample experiencing declines," notes Eatwell.[4]

Recent studies have found little empirical evidence regarding the growth effects of financial liberalization and globalization. Using a wide array of econometric tools for measuring international financial integration in 57 countries, the IMF researchers found no evidence to support the view that financial integration stimulates economic growth.[5] An interesting study by Dani Rodrik while examining three indicators of economic performance (per capita GDP growth, investment ratio in GDP, and inflation) pointed out that free capital mobility did not have any significant impact on the economies of almost 100 countries (developing and the developed) during 1975-89, which had no restrictions on the capital account. Comparing the growth performance of countries that have liberalized capital account and those that have not, the study found no evidence of the former having performed better. The study concluded that countries without capital controls have neither grown faster nor invested more and have not experienced lower inflation.

Restrictions on capital account have not necessarily led to poor economic performance. Many countries enjoyed high growth without liberalizing their capital accounts. Japan, China and South Korea are some of the examples. China demonstrates that high growth rates can be achieved without liberalization of the capital account. Can anyone buy the argument that growth rates in China would have been much higher than the present ones (over 8 per cent) had it adopted capital account liberalization? Even in Malaysia, which re-imposed capital controls in 1998 in the wake of the Southeast Asian financial crisis, the economy has grown faster than other countries in the region.

In the 1970s and 1980s, South Korea witnessed extraordinary economic growth when the government strictly controlled its capital account. The growth prospects were put in jeopardy in mid-1990s when South Korea undertook rapid financial liberalization and globalization as a precondition to join the OECD. This paved the way for reckless borrowing and lending by the Korean commercial and merchant banks along with other financial institutions that subsequently precipitated the financial crisis of 1997. It holds true for Chile, Uruguay and Argentina that rapidly liberalized their capital account in the mid-1970s. In these countries, CAL led to rapid capital flight, banking crises, large-scale bankruptcies, falling output and massive unemployment. Similarly, eruption of several financial crises in the 1990s, particularly the Southeast Asian financial crisis, significantly lowered economic growth and raised unemployment on a global scale.

To a large extent, the quality of capital flows determines the growth and productivity rates. Capital flows in the form of portfolio investment have tenuous linkages with the real economy and are speculative in nature. The bulk of portfolio investment and other speculative funds are prone to reversals with changes in the international interest rates. As financial markets are imperfect due to asymmetric information, moral hazard, herd behavior and self-fulfilling prophecies, it would be erroneous to assume that free movement of speculative capital will boost productive investments.

In the present circumstances, it has become an uphill task to establish direct linkages between FDI and economic growth if other factors such as competition policy, labor skills and policy interventions are not taken into account. In the last two decades, the attributes of FDI flows, known for their stability and spillover benefits, have changed profoundly. FDI is no longer as stable as it used to be in the past. Since bulk of FDI flows are associated with cross border mergers and acquisitions, their positive impact on the domestic economy through technological transfers and spillover effects has been significantly diluted.

One of the guiding principles that determines the impact of FDI on national economic growth is whether foreign capital complements or substitutes domestic capital. In the case of several developing countries, it has been observed that foreign investment often displaces domestic investment. In Latin America, the increase in real investment has been only about one third of the net capital inflow.[6] In fact, if one takes the Latin American region as a whole, external savings have crowded out the national savings. In New Zealand, both household and corporate savings have witnessed a steep decline since financial liberalization.[7] There is ample evidence of lower private savings rates following liberalization in Argentina, Chile, Colombia and the Philippines.[8]

There are several instances where financial liberalization and globalization policies have contributed to a consumption boom. In Mexico, the inflows sustained a boom in private consumption after its capital account was liberalized in the late 1980s. In 1992-93, capital inflows were estimated at 8 per cent of the GDP. With higher interest rates in Mexico, the international investment banks and fund managers invested billions of dollars in the financial markets and real estate, and consequently, a sharp real estate and stock market boom ensued. The higher but unrealistic valuation of stocks and real estate coupled with the appreciation of the exchange rate fuelled the consumption boom. There was a substantial hike in consumer lending after liberalization in Mexico as banks rapidly expanded credit card businesses and loans for consumer items. As a result, investment stagnated and foreign savings crowded out domestic savings. The national savings as a ratio of the GDP plummeted by more than 4 percentage points between 1989 and 1994. Mexico had to pay a high price for financial liberalization. In 1995, its GDP contracted by 7 per cent and inflation soared above 50 per cent.[9]

There is little evidence to support the view that free movement of capital will simply mean the flow of savings from capital-rich countries to capital-poor countries. The latest data on international capital flows shows that net transfer of financial resources has been predominantly towards the capital-rich countries, particularly the US. Despite the fact that global capital mobility has increased exponentially in the 1990s and real rates of return in the US are lower than other countries, the US continues to absorb nearly two-thirds of the rest of the world's surplus savings. In the eighties, the US became the world's biggest debtor nation (a net importer of capital). Since then, the US economy has become increasingly dependent on foreign capital. In fact, much of the recent increase in foreign capital has gone into the purchase of treasury bills and equities.

The orthodox economic theory postulates that free movement of capital allows international diversification of assets, thereby enhancing opportunities for savers and reducing costs for borrowers. But there is no evidence to prove that financial globalization has in any way contributed to the lowering of borrowing costs. On the contrary, real long-term interest rates were found to be higher in the 1980s. "In all the G-7 countries, real interest rates have risen sharply in the 1980s as compared with the Bretton Woods era of capital controls," finds Eatwell's study.[10] Higher interest rates, to some extent, have contributed to lower investment and reduced growth in most parts of the world. Besides, the benefits of free movement of capital have largely accrued to financiers and investors in the form of higher real interest rates. Given the minuscule number of 'global investors,' these benefits have not trickled down to the majority of the people. Needless to add, what is good for a 'global investor' may not be good for a peasant, worker, trader or small entrepreneur.

Another myth propagated by orthodox theory that financial openness provides healthy discipline for governments is based on mistaken premises. Evidence shows that there are several inherent difficulties in managing an economy with an open capital account. Premature opening of the capital account can exacerbate the existing weaknesses in the domestic financial system with catastrophic consequences on the real economy. An open capital account not only constricts countries to pursue independent monetary policies, but also a sudden change in the perception of foreign investors could plunge the domestic financial system into a crisis.

There is plenty of evidence suggesting that volatile capital flows are not only sensitive to domestic conditions in the host countries but also to macroeconomic conditions (for instance, interest rates) in the home countries. Sudden withdrawal of capital can negatively impact on the exchange and interest rates, thereby complicating economic management and threatening macroeconomic stability. As is well recognized, a domestic crisis can have a contagion effect due to higher degree of global integration of financial markets.

Since the collapse of Bretton Woods system, various types of financial crises (banking crises, currency crises or both, also known as 'twin crises') have occurred in both the developed and the developing countries. It has been estimated that nearly 100 financial crisis have occurred in the last three decades with adverse consequences on output, growth and employment. It is true that financial crises are more likely to occur in countries with weak regulatory mechanisms but countries with strong regulatory regimes have also experienced a variety of financial crises. It also needs to be pointed out that financial crises have occurred regardless of economic fundamentals. Several developed countries with sound economic fundamentals as well as 'model' economies have experienced severe banking and currency crises in the wake of financial liberalization. Savings and Loan crisis in the US as well as Mexican and Asian financial crises are shining examples.

Admittedly, financial openness is not the only causal factor responsible for the financial crisis but growing literature confirms that liberalization of capital flows has contributed to financial crises in a number of countries. In the wake of financial liberalization, currency and banking crises get intertwined. In a large number of episodes of financial crisis, particularly in the developing countries, it was observed that financial openness made countries more vulnerable to 'twin crises.' In fact, an open capital account is the prominent channel through which contagion occurs. Several studies have also corroborated the fact that there is a direct linkage between financial liberalization and the onset of financial crisis. In 1996, Kaminsky and Reinhart took a sample of 20 countries that underwent a total of 76 currency crises and 26 banking crises between 1970 and 1975 and came to the conclusion that banking and currency crises are the inevitable outcome of unbridled financial liberalization.[11] In 1998, Asli Demirguc-Kunt and Enrica Detragiache of the World Bank and the IMF studied a panel of 53 countries for the period 1980-85 and concluded that banking crises are more likely to occur in liberalized financial systems.[12] An extensive survey conducted by Williamson and Mahar found that financial liberalization was the single-most important contributory factor for causing financial crises in Argentina, Chile, Mexico, the Philippines, Thailand, Turkey, the US and Venezuela.[13] These empirical case studies have conclusively proved that financial liberalization is one of the causative elements responsible for the eruption of financial crises worldwide.

In all the episodes of financial crisis, financial liberalization (both domestic and external) preceded the crisis. To cite a few examples, Italy and France had liberalized their capital account just before the Exchange Rate Mechanism (ERM) crisis. Similarly, Mexico and the Southeast Asian countries had undertaken financial liberalization in the 1990s. Turkey and Bolivia also faced similar consequences with financial liberalization. Financial liberalization was one of the major factors that perpetuated financial crisis in the Southern cone countries namely, Argentina, Chile and Uruguay in the late 1970s and early 1980s. The costs of financial crises in these countries are estimated to be between 10 and 20 per cent of the GDP. In terms of bank defaults, closures, loss in output, unemployment and poverty, the cumulative costs of these crises have been enormous.

In comparison to the developed countries, the overall social

Box 1.2

Turkey: Limping from One Financial Crisis to Another

During the months of November-December 2000, Turkey's financial system was in deep turmoil. The overnight inter-bank interest rates climbed as high as 1700 per cent. At one point, these rates even touched 1950 per cent. Domestic interest rates almost doubled at 60 per cent. As foreign investors started selling equities, the Istanbul stock market became extremely volatile and almost lost half of its value at the beginning of the year. As witnessed in the case of the Southeast Asian financial crisis, financial flows also reversed sharply in Turkey. Fearing an impending liquidity crisis, foreign investors immediately took their money out from Turkey. The exodus of foreign funds was so sudden and swift that nearly $6 billion left the country within just 10 days. On November 22, 2000 alone, $2.5 billion left Turkey.

It is important to note that the financial turmoil in Turkey was not triggered by the macroeconomic fundamentals. The crisis was ostensibly triggered by concerns about the health of the banking system of Turkey. It all began with a criminal investigation into 10 insolvent Turkish private banks that were taken over by the government in 1999 after pumping $6 billion. The investigation led to the arrests of key bankers who were accused of siphoning money from these banks. Corrupt practices in the banking sector of Turkey are not a new phenomenon. But mismanagement and corruption in the banking sector became more rampant when the Turkish authorities began relaxing regulations and controls in the banking sector under the liberalization program started in the 1980s. The ruling elite of Turkey and their cronies misused lax banking regulations to plunder millions of dollars for their individual enrichment and aggrandizement. Many of the failed Turkish banks were involved in corrupt deals by providing unsound loans to politically well-connected people. Several banks made huge profits by

contd. on next page

borrowing foreign currencies at low rates and then using the proceeds to buy domestic assets, particularly high-yielding Turkish treasury bills. But when the interest rates dropped significantly in Turkey, these banks could not sustain such risky arbitrage activities.

Instead of welcoming positive steps by the Turkish authorities to clean up the banking sector, the financial markets started speculating on the connections between accused bankers and other banks. All kinds of rumors were afloat that other banks would also go bust. This prompted foreign investors to immediately sell off their Turkish assets and cut lending. As a result, demand for dollars increased and interest rates shot up. Fearing an imminent devaluation of the Turkish lira, as happened in the past, investors left the country hurriedly. The calm in the financial markets was only restored in the first week of December 2000 when the IMF announced a rescue package of $7.5 billion to Turkey. The loan package was the 18th such loan from IMF to Turkey, making the country the biggest recipient of IMF credit.

The victims of Turkey's crisis are both the financial sector and the real economy. Since February 19, 2001, when the Turkish lira collapsed, banks were burdened with heavy bad debts. Under the rescue package, known as the 'Istanbul approach,' several banks in Turkey have been closed down or merged with other entities. The total number of banks in Turkey has decreased from 82 at the end of 1999 to 57 in 2002.

Despite being propped up by another $12 billion IMF loan, the Turkish economy faced its worst recession since 1945. The economy declined by 9.4 per cent in 2001. A number of Turkish corporations encountered closure on account of mounting bank debts, plunging sales and lack of operating capital. While some other corporations had to sell their assets to foreign investors to pay off their huge bank debts. The country, already undergoing a strict belt-tightening disinflation program, confronted new taxes and cuts in public

contd. on next page

spending. This has severely affected the poor people of Turkey, many of whom earn less than $150 a month. Unlike other European countries, the vast majority of Turkish people live in abject poverty and almost half of the population is still dependent on agriculture. In addition, a whopping number of government jobs have been cut down. The unemployment rate has jumped from 6.3 per cent in 2000 to 10.6 per cent at the end of 2001.

The Turkish episode not only reveals the severe economic and social costs of a fragile domestic banking system operating under a lax regulatory environment but also the preeminent role of unregulated short-term financial flows in precipitating a financial crisis. Is it not a paradox that financial markets are even punishing those countries that are sincerely reforming their economies as per its diktats?

costs of financial crises have been much greater in the developing countries due to heavy burden of external indebtedness and lack of safety nets. Besides, the boom-and-bust cycles disproportionately affect the poor people. Since the financial assets and purchasing power of poor people are meager, they do not benefit in the boom phase. But the bust phase, consisting of austerity measures, brings greater misery to poor people through job losses, fall in real wages, higher inflation, higher taxes and reduced public expenditures. Indonesia, Thailand and South Korea have witnessed sharp increase in poverty levels after the financial crisis. In Indonesia alone, the proportion of people forced to live on less than $1 per day increased from 11 per cent in 1997 to 19.9 per cent in 1998, implying a staggering increase of 20 million in the ranks of the poor.[14] The Southeast Asian financial crisis has emphatically demonstrated to the world that financial globalization is a vexatious issue with numerous reverberating effects on the real economy.

The Consolidation of Global Banking Industry

The global banking industry has undergone rapid consolidation and restructuring since the 1990s. Mergers and acquisitions (M&As), privatization of state-owned banks, removal of restrictions on the entry of foreign banks and deregulation of banking industry are part of this process. In order to enhance financial competition, regulatory measures such as interest rate ceilings and credit controls have been removed. Apart from domestic pressures to liberalize the banking industry, several regional and international agreements have also given impetus to market-driven consolidation of the global banking industry. For instance, removal of the restrictions on the entry of foreign banks is an integral component of the WTO and NAFTA as well as a precondition of membership of the OECD and EU. In addition, several banking crises during the 1990s have also hastened the process. In Central and Eastern Europe (CEE) and Latin America, the domestic banking system has been rapidly transformed largely due to privatization of state-owned banks. According to the proponents of financial liberalization, increased consolidation and competition in the banking industry improves the efficiency of domestic banks and results in greater access to credit. The market driven consolidation of the global banking industry raises a number of important policy issues, some of which are discussed here.

As more and more developing countries are easing restrictions on the entry of foreign banks, the cross border M&A mania in the global banking industry has intensified. In the fierce competitive environment created by the mergers and acquisitions, big banks are swallowing each other to dominate global banking industry. Thanks to M&As, Citigroup became the largest bank in the world with assets of $1.09 trillion in 2002. Despite suffering huge losses for the past several years, Japanese banks have again bounced back to top global positions that they enjoyed in the 1980s, largely on account of M&As. Mizuho Group of Japan (a holding company formed by merger of three large banks — Fuji, Dai-Ichi Kangyo and Industrial Bank of Japan) holds the second position in the world with assets of $1.08 trillion in 2002.

The impact of allowing foreign banks to acquire stakes in the domestic banking market has been more dramatic in CEE region where most domestic banks have already become or are likely to become subsidiaries of large foreign banks. In the wake of massive privatization programs in these countries, foreign banks have rapidly taken control over the domestic banking industry. In the nine CEE states, foreign bank holdings have risen from 20 per cent of assets in 1997 to over 60 per cent by the end of 2001. In the Baltic states of Estonia, Latvia and Lithuania, foreign banks (particularly from the Scandinavian countries) captured the domestic banking market within a short span of time. In Estonia, for instance, foreign-owned banks increased their market share from 2.3 per cent in 1997 to over 97 per cent in 2000. The top three banks of Estonia —

Table 1.1: Market Share of Foreign Banks* in CEE countries
(in percentage)

Country	1996	1997	1998	1999	2000
Estonia	2.6	2.3	90.2	89.8	97.4
Latvia	NA	NA	NA	NA	69.8
Poland	16.0	18.6	27.9	65.5	65.7
Slovak Republic	13.6	26.0	25.9	31.1	65.4
Hungary	58.0	55.4	59.4	53.9	61.9
Lithuania	NA	NA	NA	NA	59.9

* Banks that are at least 50 per cent foreign-owned.
NA= Not Available.
Source: Bank Austria Creditanstalt Economics Department.

Box 1.3

China's Banking Sector and the WTO Regime

Historically, China's financial system, essentially a bank-based system, was structured to serve the needs of the planned economy. Even when liberalization program was initiated in 1978, China took special measures to protect the financial sector. The Chinese authorities put severe restrictions on the entry and operations of both domestic and foreign banks. The public sector banks in China have played a central role in mobilizing savings from public and making it available to state-owned enterprises (SOEs) and others. Although recently, the Chinese authorities have granted operational autonomy to the banks, the bulk of China's banking system is still owned by the government. The top four state-owned banks account for nearly 80 per cent of total assets.

Till now, the operations of foreign banks have been very limited with stringent geographical and business restrictions placed on them. Foreign banks in China were confined to foreign currency business, that too with foreign corporations. The earlier strategy of limited financial liberalization has been turned upside down by WTO dictated timetables for rapid liberalization in the banking, securities and insurance sectors. Several major concessions have been granted by China to foreign banks under the WTO deal. Foreign banks have been allowed to conduct all types of foreign exchange transactions with foreign clients immediately upon accession to the WTO in 2001 while there would be no geographical and client restrictions on foreign banks to operate in China by the year 2006. This would give a major boost to the foreign banks as they have been waiting to capture the banking markets of China, which have almost a trillion dollars in personal savings. In particular, foreign banks are going to capture markets in those regions (e.g., coastal regions and cities) where bulk of banking business is concentrated. Given the fact that foreign banks have considerable international exposure and can launch new products (e.g., ATM, credit card, etc) besides providing better services, they are in an

contd. on next page

advantageous position to capture China's banking businesses. Foreign banks are also going to dominate the highly lucrative trade-related businesses.

The opening up of the banking sector would pose no immediate threat to the big four state-owned banks because they have vast branch networks in both urban and rural areas. But the worst sufferers of opening up would be small and medium-sized commercial banks in China. These banks provide credit to small and medium-sized companies in China who are the engines of economic growth in China. Therefore, it seems likely that less credit would be available to small and medium-sized companies in future which, in turn, would have negative repercussions on the economic growth.

Further, by allowing foreign banks to offer banking services to residents, elites may be induced to move their savings from state-owned banks to foreign banks that can offer efficient services and new products. It has been estimated that about 10 to 15 per cent of savings in state banks would move to foreign banks. Given the fact that the survival of many SOEs depends on getting loans from the state banks, such a shift of savings could pose a severe threat to the entire economy. If such a massive shift in banking occurs within a short period, the state banks won't be able to support the SOEs, and as a result many SOEs may go bankrupt.

Undeniably, WTO agreement also offers opportunities for the Chinese banks to compete in the international financial markets. But this is unlikely to happen for two reasons. Firstly, Chinese banks do not have any exposure to international markets. Secondly, the real challenge for the Chinese banks would be to retain hold on their domestic markets, rather than looking for opportunities in international markets. Under liberalized financial system, the Chinese authorities may not be able to sustain economic growth because finance capital makes it difficult for countries to pursue independent policy making. Since the Chinese authorities are determined to go ahead with banking sector liberalization program, it remains to be seen how China would adjust to one-size-fits-all strategy.

Hansapank, Uhipank and Optiva — are all foreign-owned. In Latvia, Poland and Slovak Republic, foreign-owned banks accounted for more than 65 per cent of total market shares in 2000 (see Table 1.1). In terms of assets, over 90 per cent of Czech Republic banking sector has come under the control of foreign banks.[15] Out of a total of 41 banks in Romania, 31 were majority or fully foreign-owned in 2001.

In Latin America, similar trends are also visible. For instance, all three top banks of Mexico (Bancomer, Serfin and Banamex) have come under the control of foreign banks through M&A deals. With the takeover of Bital by a transnational bank, HSBC, the total foreign ownership in Mexican banking industry has touched 90 per cent of total banking assets. Since foreign banks had no presence in the domestic markets in the 1990, such a rapid takeover of Mexican banking industry by foreign banks has been accomplished within a few years, particularly after the 1994 currency crisis. In Brazil, foreign banks controlled 70 of country's 181 banking institutions at the end of 2001. In Peru, Venezuela and Chile, foreign banks have also acquired substantial stakes in the domestic banking markets.

In Asia, rapid consolidation of the banking industry has taken place in the aftermath of the Southeast Asian financial crisis. In several crisis-hit Asian economies, bank mergers have been carried out to make them financially viable and large enough to compete with foreign banks in the domestic markets. In Malaysia, for instance, Danamodal, a specialized institution was set up to facilitate consolidation in the banking system. By urging banks to merge voluntarily, 54 financial institutions were merged into 10 'anchor' banks in Malaysia in 1999. In South Korea, Thailand and Indonesia, similar mergers have taken place after injecting large amounts of public funds in the banking system. The other important consequence of the Southeast Asian financial crisis has been changes in the ownership of banks in the region. In almost every crisis-hit Asian country, a number of banks were nationalized (and subsequently reverted to private ownership) and restrictions were removed on the ownership of foreign banks in the domestic markets. In the case of Indonesia, South Korea and Thailand, the foreign equity participation in local banks has been raised to 100 per cent. With the result, a dramatic increase in the presence of foreign banks in these countries since the mid-1990s has taken place.

Due to rapid consolidation, the total number of banks has significantly declined throughout the world. In the case of US, the M&A activity in the banking sector received a major boost when regulations on inter-state banking were lifted. With the result, the total number of banks has decreased drastically from 18000 to less than 8000. In Estonia, the total number of banks has reduced from 42 in 1992 to just 7 in 2002. One of the negative consequences of M&A activity in the banking industry is the massive layoff of workers. On an average, between 10 and 20 per cent of workforce has been laid off in the wake of M&A deals. In Europe alone, M&A deals led to nearly 300000 job losses in the financial sector in the 1990s. The other consequence is the sharp increase in the market share of the top banks. According to *The Banker*, the assets of top 25 global banks accounted for $14.6 trillion (37 per cent) out of the top 1000 holding $39 trillion in 2001.[16] In the CEE states too, the market share of the top banks has increased. The top five banks in Estonia and Lithuania account for more than 90 per cent of total bank assets. In the Czech and Slovak Republics, the top five banks command more than 60 per cent of total assets, while in Hungary and Poland the ratio is more than 50 per cent.

It must be noted here that despite owning bulk of banking assets in the CEE and other regions, transnational banks have not become truly 'global.' The geographical spread of top 1000 banks has remained stable over the recent years. The triad — European Union, Japan and the US — accounts for nearly 60 per cent of top 1000 global banks.[17] In terms of assets, 78 per cent of the top 1000 banks belong to the triad.[18] Further, most of the top global banks are rooted in their domestic markets. Even Citigroup, considered to be a truly global bank having presence in over 100 countries, holds bulk of its assets in the US. With only 34 per cent of assets held outside the US, Citigroup is essentially a domestic US bank.

The Market Driven Global Banking versus Imperatives of Development

The rapid market driven consolidation in the global banking industry has important implications for the allocation of credit, which in turn affects economic growth. Rampant competition in the domestic financial sector due to entry of foreign banks could enhance the risks. Fearing erosion of the franchise value because of increased competition, banks and financial institutions have a natural tendency to lend more money to risky projects. Fierce competition in the banking sector has given rise to a situation where banks are increasingly resorting to speculative and risky activities (e.g., foreign exchange speculation) to reap higher profits. A study by Andrew Sheng of the World Bank found that increased competition was responsible for bank failures in Chile, Argentina, Spain and Kenya.[19]

Under a liberalized financial regime, the failure of a large bank can lead to collapse of other banks — which may be otherwise fundamentally sound — that in turn, could trigger a larger systemic risk. This risk in the banking industry is much greater than any other markets precisely due to inter-bank payment and settlement system. International banks are exposed to large amounts of cross border settlement risk because settlement of transactions takes place in different time zones. Since two national payment systems (for instance, of Japan and Switzerland) are never open at the same time, it poses the risk in the sense that if the first counterparty has delivered one side of the transaction, the other counterparty may go bankrupt and fail to honor the contract. This kind of risk is popularly known as 'Herstatt risk.' In June 1974, the Bundesbank closed down Herstatt Bank after business hours when it suffered huge foreign exchange losses. Several banks, which had paid out Deutsche Marks to Herstatt, suffered losses because its closure at this time of the day prevented them from receiving US dollars in return. It has been calculated that losses in the global currency markets due to settlement system amount to $300 million a year.

Moreover, the entry of foreign banks in the domestic market does not necessarily lead to better access to credit. Analysts have reported that in several countries the amount of real credit has actually declined in the wake of increased presence of foreign banks. Based on the study of two of the earliest transition economies, Hungary and Poland, Christian Weller established that there is a link between greater international financial competition and less real credit.[20] Christian found that while the number of financial intermediaries, particularly foreign-owned ones, grew in both economies, the amounts of real loans declined.[21] The decrease in total credit was more pronounced in Hungry. While real loans decreased by 5.2 per cent in Poland from 1990 to 1995, and by 47.5 per cent in Hungary between 1989 and 1994, the number of multinational banks increased from 0 to 14 in Poland and from 9 to 20 in Hungary.[22] These economies experienced considerable deterioration in their growth rates during this period.

While the entry of foreign banks is generally considered beneficial as they offer better quality services and sophisticated products and have 'deep pockets' to support losses, they can put domestic banks — whose long-term interests are aligned with the local economy — at a competitive disadvantage. It has been observed in some instances that rapid entry of foreign banks could stall the development of the local banking sector, as witnessed in Australia in the 1980s. By neglecting small and medium-sized enterprises (SMEs), foreign banks can even jeopardize the prospects of economic growth. If recent experiences are any guide, foreign banks have a tendency to serve the needs of less risky segments such as transnational corporations and 'cherry-picked' host country corporations. Consequently, domestic banks are left with less creditworthy segments of the banking market such as farmers, SMEs and traders. Its consequences for the real economy could be disastrous not only for the developing economies but also developed economies like the US, Germany and Japan where small and medium-sized enterprises constitute the backbone of manufacturing and services.

Since bank credit is a vital input for investment and growth, the liberalization of banking sector could also negatively affect the growth prospects, particularly of those countries which have bank-based financial systems. Increased competition could lead to cost cutting measures such as closure of bank branches, particularly in the rural and remote areas. In this context, the experience of India is worth illustrating.

India nationalized the banking sector in 1969 with an objective to transform class banking into mass banking. Banks were given targets for lending in priority sectors (such as agriculture) and were directed to offer banking services to the poor and weaker sections of the society who were neglected by the private banks. Under the nationalization drive, bank branches increased exponentially, from 8200 to over 62000. Most of the new bank branches were opened in the unbanked, rural areas. This policy regime not only helped in increasing household savings but also provided substantial invest-ments in agriculture, small and medium-sized enterprises and the informal sector. Notwithstanding widespread corruption and red-tapism, the nationalized banks significantly contributed towards the expansion of the country's agricultural and industrial base and regional development. Even the proponents of financial liberaliza-tion cannot deny the fact that the financial system was subservient to the needs of the real economy under the nationalized regime.

Since the priorities of the banks in India are now geared to-wards earning profits, substantial economic and social gains achieved during the nationalization period are fading. Since the 1990s, when the authorities initiated banking sector liberalization in India, a large number of bank branches, particularly in the rural areas, have been closed down. There is ample evidence to show that rural and agricultural credit and lending to small-scale industries and infor-mal sector have suffered negatively under the liberalized regime. The potential costs to the liberalized regime such as reduced saving and investment, particularly in rural areas, cannot be underesti-mated. Even the new thrust on microfinance programs in the rural areas of the country is unlikely to expand institutional credit if the current policy of large-scale closures of bank branches is not re-versed.

The consequences of the domestic banking reforms on growth could also be disastrous for the developed economies. In Germany, for instance, 540 Sparkassen (saving banks) along with 12 Landesbanken (state banks) are the main financiers of the Mittelstand (small and medium-sized enterprises), which consti-tutes over 95 per cent of German companies and employs nearly 70 per cent of the country's workforce. However, under the directives of EU, the Sparkassen would lose state guarantees in 2005. The removal of state guarantees would not only lead to closure of several Sparkassen but also jeopardize growth and employment prospects, as Mittelstand would encounter serious credit crunch.

South Korea and Japan enjoyed rapid economic growth and financial stability under a regime of tight credit and banking controls. In the case of South Korea, the authorities promoted their long-term industrial policy of export oriented industries by targeting financial resources towards industrial projects and providing credits at preferential rates of interest. The policy of 'strategic planning' in Japan was supported by credit controls which ensured that sufficient credit was available for priority areas. However, when South Korea and Japan introduced reforms in the banking sectors, not only their economic performance deteriorated but their financial systems also became much more fragile.

The consolidation in the global banking industry would get a major fillip with the implementation of New Basel Capital Accord (Basel II) in 2006. The Basel II replaces the 1988 Basel Accord which was initially an agreement between the G-10 countries but was later adopted by over 100 countries. The 1988 Accord required banks to maintain 8 per cent of their risk-adjusted assets as capital. The Basel II is ostensibly meant to encourage banks to align their capital more closely with underlying risk. However, the Basel II Accord could also have undesirable macroeconomic consequences and may prove counterproductive under present circumstances. Since risk-based capital requirements would encourage pro-cyclical lending behavior, it can give rise to negative macroeconomic consequences in the form of increased amplitude of business cycles. Besides, the Basel II would strengthen the competitive advantage of big transnational banks with lower levels of regulatory capital requirements. It has been estimated that big transnational banks are likely to save more than 20 per cent of regulatory capital which could provide greater impetus to the M&A activity on a global scale. The local and smaller banks in both the developed and the developing world would be the worst sufferers under Basel II Accord as they would be saddled with more stringent regulatory capital requirements.

Microfinance, Poverty Reduction and Women's Empowerment

While advocating financial liberalization, microfinance is often advocated as a panacea for poverty reduction and development. However, the success of microfinance programs in reducing poverty is extremely limited and is usually dependent on other developmental efforts which are undermined by the structural adjustment policies. Historically, women's groups and NGOs initiated microfinance programs at local levels as one component of development strategy to empower poor women. But nowadays, microfinance is no longer a localized activity. It has become a global industry, estimated to be over $10 billion. From World Bank to Citigroup, everyone has jumped onto the microfinance bandwagon. For banks and financial institutions, microfinance offers new avenues of profit making since interest rates range from 20 to 40 per cent and repayment rates are over 90 per cent, far above commercial lending. This economic logic makes the poor more attractive to banks and financial institutions, but not vice-versa. Even agricultural and consumer goods companies have jumped onto the microfinance bandwagon to penetrate the rural markets.

Despite global hard selling of microfinance as a panacea for poverty alleviation, its 'success' requires critical examination.[23] The common criterion used in measuring success of microfinance programs is loan repayment rate. No doubt, loan repayment rate is very high as compared to commercial lending but this does not explain the qualitative impact of such programs in terms of increasing flows of income, levels of employment and sustainability of businesses. Since lenders are primarily concerned with repayment of loans, vital issues related to the quality and wider socioeconomic impact of such loans have not been given due attention.

Impact studies of microfinance programs run by Grameen Bank in Bangladesh, one of the pioneers of microfinance, reveal that Grameen workers and peer group members put pressure on women borrowers for timely repayment, rather than devising a strategy of collective responsibility and borrower empowerment, as originally envisaged by the Grameen Bank. Under such pressure, many women borrowers maintain their regular repayment schedules through loan recycling (that is, paying off previous loans by acquiring new ones) which ultimately increases the debt liability of the borrower. The increased debt liability, in turn, aggravates family tensions and produces new forms of social dominance including violence on women borrowers.

Empirical studies reveal that it is not always the poorest of the poor women who get the credit. Rather, those with sizeable income and assets often corner the biggest chunk of credit. Further, studies have also reported that much of credit is used by poor women to meet consumption needs (e.g., food, health, clothing, marriage, festivals, etc.) instead of investment in businesses, thereby negating the essence of microfinance programs.

The growing over-dependence of microfinance institutions on donors is a matter of serious concern. There are very few instances where microfinance institutions have become sustainable without the support of donors. On the contrary, one finds that dependence on donors has further increased with the expansion of microfinance programs, thereby putting a question mark on the long-term financial sustainability of these institutions. This is despite the fact that most microlenders charge relatively higher interest rates, in the range of 12 to 36 per cent. Hence, a proper regulatory framework has to be chalked out for the functioning of microlenders. Otherwise, these entities would regress into an exploitative form of organized money lending with no public accountability.

The contention that microfinance as a cure-all for poverty alleviation is highly misplaced. Advocates of microfinance programs view poverty as a cash flow problem and seek its solution through credit and income-generation programs. Poverty, particularly that of women, cannot be defined only in terms of cash flow since it has strong linkages with inequitable distribution of resources, unequal power relations, illiteracy, lower wages, cuts in developmental spending and anti-poor macroeconomic policies that disproportionately affect the poor women.

It also needs to be emphasized that microfinance is not a substitute of social sector spending and anti-poverty programs. How beneficial is credit if cuts in social services continue to exacerbate women's poverty and increase their total labor hours? It is not being argued that credit has no role in alleviating poverty but what can women do with a few dollars if they do not get education, health services, training, and child care facilities? Women's empowerment is much more than credit and income generation programs. For instance, in the rural context, women's control and ownership over land can play a crucial role not only in economic betterment but also in terms of social and political empowerment, as land is a symbol of political power and social status.

Microfinance programs have to be visualized in the context of new global economic order as liberalization, privatization and globalization policies have led to job losses in the formal sector, decline in social sector spending, and growing unemployment. In this scenario, the last option left for the poor women is self-employment, which microfinance aims to promote. But poor women are placed at an extremely disadvantageous position in the market. How can products of poor women compete with those of big business houses and transnational corporations, which not only have strong financial backing but also spend millions on advertising, brand selling and marketing. Until and unless the poor women are provided access to market information, technology, management and marketing skills, their economic ventures would remain uncompetitive. Since the efficacy of microfinance programs is not independent of other developmental interventions, it could at best be one of the components of a wider developmental agenda.

Concluding Remarks

The arguments in favor of financial globalization are not well founded. Empirical evidence militates against the orthodox thinking that unfettered global capital flows can promote investment and growth besides better allocation of resources and deepening of financial markets. In the light of recent experiences, very few can assert that global capital flows provide immense benefits to countries, particularly the developing ones. The benefits of global capital mobility have only accrued to a minuscule number of 'global investors' and financiers. While the costs are enormous because volatile capital flows can cause sharp swings in real exchange rates and financial markets thereby engendering instability in the financial system and the real economy.

The recurring financial crisis underscores the necessity for effective, constructive and well-coordinated regulation of financial markets. Currently, the discourse has shifted to 'sequencing' and 'orderly' financial liberalization and globalization. These approaches emphasize the timing and sequencing of capital account liberalization and identify the real cause of financial crises in the domain of weak domestic financial system, particularly the banking system.[24] But such approaches suffer from serious limitations in terms of application for various reasons. There seems to be no consensus on what is an 'orderly' financial liberalization and capital account liberalization — what may be an appropriate timing of liberalization in one country may not be for another. Besides, in the real world, powerful interests and lobbies see to it that issues pertaining to pace and sequencing of reforms are consigned to the backyard.

The time has come to seriously contest the ideological moorings on which the agenda of financial liberalization and globalization is rooted.

Notes and References

1. Stanley Fischer, "Capital Account Liberalization and the Role of the IMF," in *Should the IMF Pursue Capital-Account Convertibility?*, Essays in International Finance, No. 207, International Finance Section, Department of Economics, Princeton University, Princeton, May 1998, pp. 2-3.

2. World Bank, *Globalization, Growth, and Poverty: Building an Inclusive World Economy*, Oxford University Press, New York, 2002, p. 41.

3. John Eatwell, *International Financial Liberalization: The Impact on World Development*, Discussion Paper Series, No. 12, UNDP, New York, 1997.

4. Ibid., p. 20.

5. Hali J. Edison, Ross Levine, Luca Ricci and Torsten Slok, *Capital Account Liberalization and Economic Performance: Survey and Synthesis*, IMF Working Paper 02/120, IMF, Washington, 2002; and Hali J. Edison, Ross Levine, Luca Ricci and Torsten Slok, *International Financial Integration and Economic Growth*, NBER Working Paper 9164, National Bureau of Economic Research, Cambridge, 2002.

6. Robert Devlin, Ricardo Ffrench-Davis and Stephany Griffith-Jones, "Surges in Capital Flows and Development: An Overview of Policy Issues in the Nineties," in Ricardo Ffrench-Davis and Stephany Griffith-Jones (eds.), *Coping With Capital Surges: The Return of Finance to Latin America*, Lynne Rienner, Boulder, 1995.

7. Simon Chappel, *Financial Liberalization in New Zealand, 1984-90*, Discussion Paper No. 35, UNCTAD, Geneva and New York, March 1991.

8. John Williamson and Molly Mahar, *A Survey of Financial Liberalization*, Essays in International Finance, No. 211, International Finance Section, Department of Economics, Princeton University, Princeton, November 1998, p. 52.

9. Manuel R. Agosin, "Liberalize, but Discourage Short-term Flows," in Isabelle Grunberg, (ed.), *Perspectives on International Financial Liberalization*, Discussion Paper Series, No. 15, Office of Development Studies, UNDP, New York, 1998, p. 5.

10. John Eatwell, op. cit., p. 16.

11. Graciela L. Kaminsky and Carmen M. Reinhart, "The Twin Crises: The Causes of Banking and Balance-of-Payments Problems," *The American Economic Review*, Vol. 89, No. 3, June 1999, pp. 473-500.

12. Asli Demirguc-Kunt and Enrica Detragiache, *Financial Liberalization and Financial Fragility*, IMF Working Paper 98/83, IMF, Washington, 1998.

13. John Williamson and Molly Mahar, op. cit.

14. Nick Beams, "'Free Market' Program Boost World Poverty," International Committee of the Fourth International, (via Internet), June 8, 1999.

15. Colin Jones, "Foreign Banks Move In," *The Banker*, September 2001, p. 130.

16. Stephen Timewell, "Top 1000 World Banks," *The Banker*, July 2002, p. 172.

17. Ibid., p. 203.

18. Ibid., p. 200.

19. Andrew Sheng, *Bank Restructuring: Lessons from the 1980s*, World Bank, Washington, 1996.

20. Christian Weller, *The Connection Between More Multinational Banks and Less Real Credit in Transition Economies*, Working Paper B8, Center for European Integration Studies, Bonn, 1999.

21. Ibid., p. 8.

22. Ibid., p. 2.

23. For a critical analysis of microfinance programs in the new global setting, see Kavaljit Singh and Daphne Wysham, "Micro-credit: Band-aid or Wound?," *The Hindustan Times*, January 29, 1997; Kavaljit Singh, "Microcredit Misses the Target," *Indian Express*, May 26, 1997; and Kavaljit Singh, "Microcredit: From Sandals to Suits?," *PIRG Update*, Delhi, July 1997.

24. See, for instance, Bernhard Fischer and Helmut Reisen, *Towards Capital Account Convertibility*, OECD Development Centre Policy Brief No. 4, OECD, Paris, 1992; Deena Khatkhate, "Timing and Sequencing of Financial Sector Reforms: Evidence and Rationale," *Economic and Political Weekly*, July 11, 1998, pp. 1831-1840; and Sebastian Edwards, "A Capital Idea?: Reconsidering a Financial Quick Fix," *Foreign Affairs*, May/June 1999, pp. 18-22.

CHAPTER 2

Global Rules on Investment: Rules for Whom?

We are no longer writing the rules of interaction among separate national economies. We are writing the constitution of a single global economy.

Renato Ruggiero
former Director General, WTO

THOUGH there are over 2100 binding agreements that contain provisions related to foreign investment at the bilateral, regional (e.g., NAFTA, EU, and MERCOSUR) and sectoral levels, there is no comprehensive multilateral agreement on foreign investment. As discussed in detail in this chapter, past attempts at establishing a multilateral investment regime through various fora failed miserably. In the 1990s, efforts to launch global investment rules intensified. However, with the collapse of negotiations on Multilateral Agreement on Investment (MAI) at the OECD in the late 1990s, renewed efforts were made to establish global investment rules in the World Trade Organization (WTO).

At the First Ministerial Conference of the WTO held in Singapore in December 1996, a proposal for multilateral negotiations on investment along with competition policy, government procurement and trade facilitation was mooted. However, strong resistance by some developing countries (particularly India) led to a compromise whereby a Working Group on Trade and Investment was set up under the aegis of WTO to examine the relationship between trade and investment issues. The Working Group has been given a mandate to examine the constituents of an investment framework in terms of scope and definition, transparency, non-discrimination, modalities for pre-establishment commitments based on a GATS-style positive list, development provisions, exceptions and balance of payments safeguards, consultation and the settlement of disputes between member-countries. The task of Working Group is purely analytical and exploratory, with no mandate to negotiate new rules.

While the Working Group on Trade and Investment was examining the issue, the EU with the tacit support of other developed countries pushed the investment issue for negotiations at the Fourth Ministerial Conference of the WTO held in Doha in 2001. The Doha Ministerial Declaration, also known as Doha Development Agenda, recognized "the case for a multilateral framework to secure transparent, stable and predictable conditions for long-term cross-border investment, particularly foreign direct investment." The Declaration further stated that "negotiations will take place after the Fifth Session of the Ministerial Conference on the basis of a decision to be taken, by explicit consensus, at that Session on modalities of negotiations." But developed countries conveniently interpreted it as a mandate to launch negotiations on investment at the Cancun Conference in September 2003.

The principal demandeurs of investment rules in the WTO include EU, Japan, Canada, South Korea and Costa Rica. They are seeking a comprehensive investment agreement which would include provisions such as National Treatment (meaning that countries should treat foreign investors in the same manner as they treat domestic investors), Most Favored Nation (MFN) Treatment, complete ban on performance requirements (conditions imposed by countries such as technology transfer, export obligations, local content requirements, preference to local people in employment, off loading of shares to local population), and a dispute settlement mechanism to resolve disputes arising from investment issues. What is perplexing is that supporting countries are pushing their agenda without even arriving at a consensus on basic issues such as scope and definition of investment.

As investment issues criss-cross several sectors of economy, the consequences of investment rules at the WTO could be more detrimental than the existing agreements. If history is any guide, most investment agreement proposals are attempts at disciplining those regulatory measures which negatively discriminate foreign investors in the host countries. Global investment rules would not only bind member-countries to pursue indiscriminate investment liberalization but it would also significantly reduce the space for countries to maneuver investment policies to suit their specific conditions.

After the collapse of the MAI negotiations, the Working Group on Trade and Investment at the WTO remains the only multilateral forum where investment issues are under deliberation. Notwithstanding the collapse of Cancun Conference, supporting countries are employing myriad strategies to force consensus on investment issues. Thus, it would be naïve to think that the prospects for comprehensive global rules on investment have receded.

Regulation of Foreign Investment

Unlike trade, foreign investment is a much more politically sensitive issue since it essentially means exercising control over ownership of national assets and resources. In spite of liberalization of domestic investment rules over the decades, every country has used a variety of regulations to control foreign investment depending on its stage of development. Both the developed and the developing countries have imposed a host of regulations on foreign investment to meet the wider objectives of economic policy, particularly those related to national development. Traditionally, control on foreign investment vested with national governments. When a foreign investor enters a host country, it is required to follow the regulatory measures of that country. The State has the right to regulate the activities of foreign investors operating within its sovereign territory. The right to regulate foreign investment is delineated in the Resolution on Permanent Sovereignty Over Natural Resources approved by the UN General Assembly on December 14, 1962 which upheld permanent sovereignty over natural wealth and resources as a basic constituent of the right to self-determination. While conferring the right to retain control over economies, the Resolution emphasized that foreign investment should not be subject to conditions that are contrary to the interests of the recipient states.

In the post-war period, regulations were imposed on foreign investment due to past experiences where foreign firms not only indulged in restrictive and predatory business practices but also interfered in the domestic political affairs of the host countries. Consequently, several countries undertook measures like nationalization and appropriation of assets of foreign companies in the aftermath of their independence from colonial rule.

National treatment (pre- and post-establishment stage) happens to be the most controversial issue. Leave aside developing countries, it took more than two decades for OECD member-countries to accept the right of establishment even after signing the Code of Liberalisation of Capital Movements in 1961. Several countries have devised special measures for foreign investors (both negative and positive) to distinguish between foreign and domestic investors. The discriminatory forms of regulatory measures on

Kavaljit Singh

foreign investment vary from country to country. For instance, host countries often impose pre-admission regulations on foreign investment. Such restrictions could include screening all foreign investment on case-by-case basis, not allowing foreign investment in certain sectors of economy (for instance, telecommunications, aviation, media, atomic energy among others), and putting general and sectoral equity limits on foreign investment.

Concerned with sovereignty issues, the rationale behind pre-admission regulations is to ensure that foreign investors do not control productive and strategic sectors of the economy. It is important to stress here that the pre-admission regulations are not confined to the developing and the under-developed countries. Several developed countries (for instance, the US and Japan) have extensively imposed pre-admission regulations on foreign investment and many of them still regulate the entry of foreign investment in strategic sectors such as media, atomic energy, telecommunications and aviation. In fact, a large number of existing bilateral investment treaties reserves the right of the host countries to regulate the entry of foreign investors. Contrary to popular belief, rapid economic development has occurred amidst tight regulations on the entry of foreign investments in the two most successful cases of the post World War II period, namely, Japan and South Korea. China — the latest 'success story'— too has imposed stringent pre-admission restrictions on foreign investment including screening, negative list and sectoral limits.

In addition, there are post-admission restrictions which are imposed once the foreign investor enters the host country. Designed to maximize economic gains from foreign investment, these restrictions may include compulsory joint ventures with domestic counterparts; restrictions on remittance of profits, royalty and technical fees; additional taxes; and performance requirements

(conditions imposed on investors such as local content requirements, export obligations, preference to local people in employment, location of an industry in a backward region and mandatory
technology transfer).

Performance requirements deserve special mention here because developed countries have been advocating their elimination
on the ground that these are inefficient and distortionary thereby
hampering foreign investment and economic growth. On the contrary, evidence suggests that performance requirements such as
local content requirements and technology transfer help in establishing industrial linkages upstream and downstream and contribute significantly towards economic development of the host country. In the absence of local content requirements, a foreign corporation is likely to source many inputs from outside which could
impede the development of local clusters in the host countries. It is
a well established fact that TNCs, particularly those which have
very high levels of intra-firm trade, manipulate transfer pricing to
avoid taxes. With the help of transfer pricing, TNCs can underprice
imports of inputs thereby circumventing tariff restrictions in the
host countries. Since many developing countries lack the capacity
to check abuse of transfer pricing, local content requirements could
serve as an alternative mechanism to curb such manipulations.

What is perplexing is that developed countries had extensively
used performance requirements when they were in their initial
stage of development and were net importers of capital. As documented by Ha-Joon Chang, the US used a variety of performance
requirements including restrictions on foreign ownership of agricultural land and ban on employment of foreign workers by foreign
companies.[1] Not long ago, other developed countries such as UK,
Italy, Canada, France and Japan had also relied upon a variety of
performance requirements on foreign investment. In automobile

industry, for instance, Italy imposed 75 per cent local content rule on the Mitsubishi Pajero, the US imposed a 75 per cent local content rule on the Toyota Camry and the UK 90 per cent on the Nissan Primera.[2] While Australia had imposed a 85 per cent local content rule on automobiles until 1989.[3]

In India too, the authorities have imposed performance requirements in the form of export obligations on TNCs to ensure that the corporations earn enough foreign exchange to balance the foreign exchange outgo via repatriation of profits, royalty and other payments. For instance, Pepsico was allowed to operate in India in 1989 with the performance requirement that it will export products worth 50 per cent of its total turnover, each year for 10 years. In addition, at least 40 per cent of this export obligation has to be met by selling the company's own manufactured products.[4] Similar performance requirements have been imposed by other developing countries as well.

However, investigations have revealed that foreign investors make all kinds of false promises to honor performance requirements in order to gain entry into the host country. Once they step in, they show scant regard for fulfilling performance requirements. Several instances have been reported where foreign investors have openly flouted their post-admission commitments in the host countries. For instance, Coca-Cola has openly violated its commitment to divest 49 per cent of its equity to Indian public after five years of its operation.[5] Unfortunately, the regulatory authorities in the host countries often refuse to take any action as it may deter foreign investors from investing in the country. This issue has grave developmental ramifications, and therefore, should not be neglected by the policy makers of the host countries.

In the context of investment liberalization, countries have also started offering incentives to foreign investors in the form of tax holidays, exemption of duties, direct subsidies, loan guarantees and export credits. Many of these incentives are often tied to performance requirements. The capital exporting countries use financial incentives in the form of loan guarantees and export credit to support the ventures of their corporations while the capital importing countries offer tax holidays to attract foreign investments in their countries. Whereas, at present, there are no effective rules at the international level to discipline the use of investment incentives.

History of Investment Rules

The dominant perception that the exponential growth in foreign investment in recent years has given an impetus to launch global investment rules does not hold true. The first attempt to establish global rules on foreign investment was made in the immediate post World War II period. In 1948, the draft Charter to establish an International Trade Organization (ITO) was presented at a meeting in Havana. The ITO was meant to be the third institution for promoting post-war economic cooperation along with the International Monetary Fund and the World Bank. The ITO was conceptualized so as to boost trade liberalization within a broader developmental and regulatory framework. The draft Charter covered provisions beyond trade disciplines under Articles 11 and 12 to address foreign direct investment issues. In addition, it contained rules on restrictive business practices, commodity agreements, employment and agriculture. Had the Havana Charter been ratified, the ITO would have played a decisive role in the investment policies of the governments worldwide.

Earlier proposals on the Charter by the US granted extensive rights to foreign investors in terms of national treatment and MFN treatment. But these measures were strongly opposed by other countries. For instance, Czechoslovakia declined to grant German investors the same status as investors from other countries. As a result, the US had to dilute several rights which were granted to foreign investors in its earlier proposals. The Charter also faced the wrath of the US corporations due to provisions under Chapter V regulating anti-competitive policies of private businesses. In comparison to the present situation, the scope of investment policies under the Havana Charter was rather limited. For instance, the Charter did not incorporate any rules related to performance requirements and dispute settlement mechanism between governments and foreign investors.

In spite of the fact that the US government was one of the driving forces behind the Havana Charter, the US Congress refused to ratify it. Consequently, the proposal for establishing ITO was given up and the General Agreement on Tariffs and Trade (GATT) was launched as a temporary measure. For nearly four decades since its inception, GATT never brought investment issues under its rubric and prudently maintained the dividing line between trade and investment issues. It was only at the Uruguay Round of the GATT negotiations from 1986 to 1994 that the issue of investment was brought within its framework.

Failure to establish ITO was one of the major reasons which facilitated a shift from multilateral to bilateral investment agreements. In the 1950s and 60s, bilateral investment agreements were the dominant instruments of investment agreements. In those decades, a majority of bilateral investment agreements were geared towards protecting foreign investors against the threat of expropriation as many developing countries had undertaken nationalization measures in the aftermath of independence from colonial rule. In 1966, the International Centre for Settlement on Investment

Disputes (ICSID) was set up in the World Bank to facilitate the settlement of disputes between governments or between investors and governments. ICSID provides a mechanism through which host countries, home countries and foreign investors can agree to submit investment disputes to Third Party arbitration.

In the sixties and the seventies, international investment negotiations shifted to other fora. Big capital exporting countries led by the US started initiating discussions on investment issues at the OECD, whose membership at that time consisted of the developed world and most of its member-countries were in favor of a liberalized investment regime. As a result, two Codes — Code of Liberalization of Capital Movements and the Code of Liberalization of Current Invisible Operations — were enacted to encourage member-countries to liberalize restrictions on the cross-border movement of capital. Although the Codes were comprehensive and binding, yet the provisions related to the rights and obligations of foreign investors were not included. OECD also attempted to bring investor protection issues in the 1960s with a multilateral convention on the protection of foreign property but it was not adopted. An attempt to enact a non-binding code for transnational corporations at the OECD began in the seventies. In 1976, the Guidelines for Multinational Enterprises was adopted by OECD member-countries, largely in response to the Code of Conduct on TNCs then under negotiation at the UN.

On the other hand, the developing countries started raising investment issues with an entirely different perspective at the United Nations in the 1970s. The UN became the obvious choice for the developing countries to raise international investment issues since it ensured equal voting rights for member-countries in the General Assembly. The drive to address investment issues at the UN originated from the bitter experiences of several developing countries that were the victims of unwarranted meddling by the foreign investors in their domestic political affairs. One of the notorious examples was the International Telephone and Telegraph's (ITT) efforts to overthrow the democratically elected Salvador Allende government in Chile in the early 1970s. When similar instances of TNCs intransigence in other countries came to notice, the Group of Eminent Persons was constituted in 1972 to study the activities of the TNCs in the host countries. Later, the United Nations Commission on Transnational Corporations and the Center on Transnational Corporations were set up by the Economic and Social Council of the UN to conduct extensive research on investment issues. These initiatives were geared towards drafting a UN Code of Conduct on Transnational Corporations to curb abuse of corporate power and establish guidelines for corporate behavior in the host countries. In fact, the Code was an integral part of a broader initiative to launch a New International Economic Order (NIEO) for addressing the concerns of the developing world.

When drafting of the Code began in 1977, it was supposed to cover only the activities of transnational corporations but it later incorporated the conduct of governments as well. The 1986 draft of the Code contained extensive provisions regulating the entry and operations of transnational corporations in the host country. Concerned with the fact that the Code was unlikely to serve the interests of capital exporting countries, the US persuaded other developed countries to block the draft Code of Conduct at the UN. The Code was not approved and the UNCTC was dissolved in 1992. Since then, the work on investment issues has been carried out by the Program on Transnational Corporations of the UNCTAD with an entirely opposite agenda of promoting foreign investment. At the Earth Summit in 1992, another attempt was made to introduce regulation of TNCs under the auspices of the UN. But the developed countries along with corporate lobbies scuttled the move to incorporate environmental regulation of corporations in the Agenda 21. With the ascendancy of neoliberal ideology, the tide had started to turn against the regulation of TNCs.

UN initiatives also lost momentum in the eighties when excessive build up of external loans triggered the debt crisis in the developing world, as many countries were unable to service their huge external debt. The debt crisis of the 1980s paved the way for liberalization of investment rules as part of structural adjustment programs supported by the IMF and the World Bank. The drying up of commercial bank lending forced developing countries to open their doors to foreign investment. As a result, the developing countries that had once nationalized foreign companies started wooing foreign investors.

Initiatives at the UN did not deter the US from aggressively pursuing the investment liberalization agenda. The US not only negotiated bilateral investment agreements to secure its investment interests, it also started pursuing the investment liberalization agenda in non-UN fora where it was confident of maneuvering the outcome. Under the aegis of the Joint Development Committee of the IMF and the World Bank, the US launched discussions on the distortionary effects of investment regulations (such as performance requirements) in the host countries. These discussions provided an impetus for the enunciation of TRIMs. In the World Bank, the discussions on investment disputes led to the establishment of Multilateral Investment Guarantee Agency (MIGA) in 1988. The Agency was set up to encourage flow of private investment to the developing countries by guaranteeing the investment of foreign corporations against risks like civil war, currency restrictions, nationalization, etc.

Since the GATT (unlike the OECD) had provisions to make the rules binding among member-countries, the US returned to the GATT negotiations to push the investment liberalization agenda. Despite its failure to include investment in the Tokyo Round negotiations during 1973-79, the US remained resolute in pushing a comprehensive agreement on investment at the GATT. In the early 1980s, the US proposed a work program at GATT to include both trade in services and trade-related performance requirements imposed on foreign investors with the sole aim of addressing investment issues. But it was vehemently opposed by the developing countries, particularly India and Brazil. However, the possibility of including trade in services and investment issues at GATT negotiations became quite apparent in the mid-1980s as the opposition from developing countries waned due to bilateral trade pressures from the US as well as domestic pressures to liberalize investment regimes. The ambiguities created by the GATT ruling on the Foreign Investment Review Agency of Canada also gave momentum to the negotiations on TRIMs. The GATT panel found that the Agency's decision to screen investment proposals and impose certain performance requirements (e.g., local content) on foreign investment were in violation of Article III: 4 of GATT (National Treatment). By incorporating TRIMs and General Agreement on Trade in Services (GATS) in the Final Act of the Uruguay Round, the developed countries were successful in bringing investment issues under the ambit of GATT.

The 1990s witnessed the emergence of regional initiatives on investment liberalization. In 1991, negotiations also took place among US, Canada and Mexico to launch North American Free Trade Agreement (NAFTA). In many aspects, NAFTA was an extension to Mexico of the Canada-US Free Trade Agreement. Formally established in 1994, NAFTA contains comprehensive investment measures which are discussed in the succeeding pages. The maximum number of bilateral investment treaties were also negotiated during the 1990s.

To circumvent opposition from the developing countries, the developed countries started investment negotiations under the aegis of the OECD in the early 1990s when the neoliberal doctrine was at its zenith. In those times, a thorough liberalization of controls on foreign investment was not only considered desirable but also a necessary precondition for economic development. Trade and investment issues were deemed complementary to advance the global system of production. It is in this context that the US had called upon the OECD to launch a comprehensive binding investment treaty known as Multilateral Agreement on Investment (MAI) which included heavy dose of investment liberalization, protection of investors and a dispute resolution mechanism. Since most OECD member-countries had already liberalized investment rules, opposition to MAI was not expected. Twenty-nine member-countries of the OECD participated in the negotiations on the MAI from 1995 to 1998. In 1997, the OECD also identified certain countries (Argentina, Brazil, Chile, Hong Kong, China and the Slovak Republic) as likely candidates for accession and invited them to take part as observers at the MAI negotiations. The three Baltic countries — Estonia, Latvia and Lithuania — were later invited to join as observers.

The MAI definition of 'investment' was even broader than that adopted in Chapter 11 of NAFTA. Despite high degree of consensus among member-countries on the principles of MAI, questions were raised about the timing and preferred venue for such negotiations. In particular, the European Union and Canada were in favor of WTO as the venue for MAI because it could offer an enforceable dispute resolution mechanism. Initially, the US was not in favor of shifting the venue to WTO but eventually it supported the proposal with the caveat that Canada, the European Union and Japan should reaffirm their support for negotiations of MAI at the OECD.

While the Working Group on Trade and Investment made slow progress at the WTO, the differences among the OECD member-countries on MAI started unfolding in 1997. In spite of a consensus on the broad parameters of the agreement that included investor protection, national treatment and an extensive dispute settlement process encompassing disputes between investors and governments, disagreements cropped up on certain issues which remained unresolved. Differences among member-countries on specific issues such as Helms-Burton Act and the demand for exemption from national treatment for culture raised by France made it well nigh impossible to meet the deadlines.

In the midst of MAI negotiations, the US Parliament enacted the Cuban Liberty and Democratic Solidarity Act — popularly known as Helms-Burton Act — in 1996. The Act empowered US citizens and corporations whose property was expropriated by the Cuban government after January 1, 1959 to claim damages against anybody who transacts in their former property. The Act also prohibited entry into the US by persons who transact in confiscated property. This Act became a bone of contention between US, EU and Canada in the middle of the MAI negotiations. The underlying problem was that the Act operated extra-territorially and discriminated against foreign investors from non-US countries operating in Cuba. After the EU filed a complaint against the US over the Helms-Burton Act in the WTO, the scope of the Act was significantly constricted. By then, France had already withdrawn from the MAI negotiations. In addition, widespread popular opposition to the MAI by the NGOs, trade unions and others stalled the negotiations and the MAI was finally shelved at the OECD in November 1998.

Investment Issues under NAFTA: Some Lessons

Some developed countries are hell bent on pushing negotiations on international investment rules at the WTO, without learning anything from past experiences, viz., NAFTA and MAI. It is important to highlight here that a substantive part of investment commitments pertaining to NAFTA was simply lifted and extended to the MAI. Formulation of MAI at OECD was doomed because of its blanket approach towards investment liberalization and the secretive manner in which negotiations took place. Nevertheless, the MAI experience has many lessons to offer, the most important being that an international investment agenda which is exclusively aimed at serving the interests of foreign investors is destined to be a failure.

Though MAI was finally shelved, yet several cases filed by private corporations under the NAFTA regime are a pointer to how the agreement severely restricts the ability of governments to pursue public policies. Private corporations from NAFTA member-countries have exploited the provisions of the agreement to challenge those regulatory measures that infringe on their investment rights. The growing conflict between private corporations and regulators is the outcome of the investment provisions under Chapter 11 of the NAFTA which entails non-discriminatory treatment to foreign investors.

NAFTA restricts a wider range of performance requirements than those listed under the TRIMs agreement of the WTO. For instance, NAFTA prohibits domestic equity requirements, export performance requirements and requirements to transfer technology, production know-how or other proprietary knowledge for investments. Analysts have surmised that negotiators are likely to look into the NAFTA framework while formulating an agreement on investment at the WTO.[6] Hence, it becomes imperative to examine Chapter 11 of NAFTA which contains the most comprehensive rules on foreign investment.

The Chapter 11 of NAFTA has four main components:

(i) Scope of Application: Article 1101 deals with the coverage of provisions of NAFTA encompassing the geographical spread of the agreement (i.e., Canada, the US and Mexico). NAFTA adopts a very broad, asset-based definition of investment extending beyond FDI. It includes portfolio investments, debt finance and real estate.

(ii) Investment Liberalization: Under Articles 1102, 1103, 1104 and 1106, specific measures related to investment liberalization have been stipulated. Designed to ensure non-discriminatory treatment, foreign investors have been given National Treatment and MFN Treatment, which extend to both pre-admission and post-admission stages. Unlike GATS, NAFTA adopts a 'top-down' approach which means that commitments cover all economic sectors unless specifically exempted by the submission of a negative list by a NAFTA member-country. The commitments under NAFTA include prohibition on the use of certain performance requirements (for instance, technology transfer requirements) by member-countries. Article 1106 restricts the capacity of member-countries to link the use of incentives to certain performance requirements.

(iii) Investment Protection: Like bilateral investment agreements, NAFTA also contains rules related to investment protection under Articles 1110 and 1105. It incorporates strong guarantees of investment protection though the threat of expropriation of foreign investment has receded. Article 1110 does not allow nationalization or expropriation of foreign investment except for a public purpose. To offset the possibility of expropriation, NAFTA has in-built obligation to compensate the foreign investor of a NAFTA member-country. Article 1110 also provides an obligation to compensate when state regulatory measures "tantamount to nationalization." But there is no clear definition in NAFTA as to what constitutes this type of indirect expropriation. Article 1105 also stipulates a minimum standard of treatment "in accordance with international law, including fair and equitable treatment and full protection and security" for investors. Yet the NAFTA text does not clearly define as to what constitute "fair and equitable treatment" and "full protection and security."

(iv) Dispute Settlement: This section deals with the procedures relating to the settlement of investment disputes in the eventuality of violation of rules. In addition to the normal state-to-state dispute resolution mechanism, Chapter 11 also incorporates investor-to-state dispute resolution process. An investor of a NAFTA member-country can take legal action against violation of any of the provisions in Section A of Chapter 11. This is a major departure from other existing investment agreements. The investor-to-state dispute resolution mechanism under NAFTA has become controversial since foreign investors take recourse to it frequently.

Since its inception in 1994, NAFTA has been mired by a host of controversies. Although a majority of controversies relate to investor-to-state dispute settlement mechanism, but some pertain to conflicting interpretations and undefined areas of investment liberalization and protection measures thereby providing a leeway for its abuse. Most galling is the interpretation of the concept of 'expropriation' which, in reality, could restrict the ability of governments to carry out social and developmental measures that adversely affect the businesses of foreign investors. Since a listing of all litigations under Chapter 11 is beyond the scope of this book, four representative cases are cited here to highlight the conflicting interpretations of its several investment related Articles.

1. Metalclad Corporation vs United Mexican States: The US company, Metalclad Corporation, acquired land in order to establish a waste landfill in the Mexican Municipality of Guadalcazar. In 1993, Metalclad was granted permission to construct a waste landfill and construction work began at the site. However, the state government and local bodies opposed the project on mandatory environmental safety requirements. As a result, the company was asked to apply for a municipal construction permit. The company applied for a permit and completed the landfill in 1995. But the Municipality of Guadalcazar refused to entertain Metalclad's application for a permit and consequently the Governor of the State issued an ecological decree prohibiting the use of waste landfill. At the NAFTA Tribunal, the company argued that Mexico breached Articles 1105 (Minimum Standard of Treatment) and 1110 (Expropriation) of NAFTA. The Tribunal decided that Mexico had breached the stipulated obligations and awarded $16.7 million in damages to Metalclad in August 2000.

2. Ethyl Corporation vs Government of Canada: In April 1997, the Canadian Government banned the import and transport of MMT, a potentially toxic gasoline additive, on environmental grounds. The ban did not, however, prohibit the production and sale of MMT in Canada. Ethyl Corporation, a US company, was an importer and distributor of MMT in Canada. The company sued Canada under Chapter 11 of NAFTA for $251 million for the "expropriation" of its "property" and the "damage" to its "good reputation" caused by the public debates. The corporation filed the suit on the ground that the ban breached Articles 1102 (National Treatment), 1106 (Performance Requirements) and 1110 (Expropriation). While anticipating an adverse decision, Canada agreed to settle the dispute in July 1998. Under the settlement, the Canadian government lifted the ban on MMT and agreed to pay $13 million in compensation to Ethyl Corporation and publicly announced that "MMT poses no health risk." The settlement took place in the midst of NGO campaign against the MAI.

3. S.D. Myers Inc. vs Government of Canada: Another US company, S.D. Myers Inc., engaged a Canadian entity to transport hazardous waste (PCB) from Canada to its treatment plants in Ohio. The company claimed that Canada's blanket banning of PCB exports from November 1995 to February 1997 breached Articles 1102 (National Treatment), 1105 (Minimum Standard of Treatment), 1106 (Performance Requirements) and 1110 (Expropriation). In November 2000, the NAFTA Tribunal pronounced the verdict that Canada had breached the first two claims but found no violation of Article 1110 on expropriation. The Tribunal ordered Canada to pay $50 million to the company in 2000.

4. Methanex vs United States: In 1999, a Canadian corporation, Methanex, filed a Chapter 11 suit against the US because the State of California had decided to phase out a cancer causing gasoline additive known as MBTE. The decision to ban MBTE was based on a study undertaken by the University of California which found that there were significant risks related to water contamination due to the use of MBTE. Methanex filed the suit under Chapter 11 on the ground that the measure violated Articles 1105 (Minimum Standard of Treatment) and 1110 (Expropriation) and claimed damages of $970 million. The United States vehemently opposed the claim by pointing to the detrimental impact on the regulatory autonomy of the NAFTA member-countries. It is noteworthy that till the Methanex case, the US was generally opposed to clarifications on Chapter 11.

The above-mentioned cases not only reveal the inherent

shortcomings of Chapter 11 but also raise the issue of regulatory autonomy to deal with environmental and developmental issues. In the background of such shortcomings, the NAFTA member-countries under the aegis of the NAFTA Free Trade Commission (FTC) agreed to limit the application of some of the Articles under Chapter 11.

To sum up, the experience of NAFTA highlights the inherent difficulties in pursuing an investment liberalization agenda within a binding treaty that is limited to only three member-countries. One can well-imagine the intricacies to be encountered once an international agreement on investment incorporating similar provisions is formulated at a heterogeneous conclave like WTO with 148 member-countries.

Investment Measures Under the Existing WTO Regime

Though there are no comprehensive rules on foreign investment under the present WTO regime, investment related provisions are contained in a number of existing agreements. These provisions were introduced during the Uruguay Round of GATT negotiations.

1. Trade Related Investment Measures (TRIMs) Agreement: This agreement came into effect on January 1, 1995 as part of the Uruguay Round of negotiations. It was enacted to address trade related investment measures. The Agreement did not define TRIMs, but provided an illustrative list to abolish investment measures that adversely affect trade such as requirements on domestic content and the balancing of trade between imports and exports. As mentioned earlier, TRIMs were included in the Uruguay Round negotiations largely at the insistence of the developed countries, while many developing countries, including India, opposed it on the ground that domestic content is useful and a necessary tool of economic development.

Under the TRIMs agreement, existing GATT disciplines relating to national treatment (Article III) and the prohibition of quantitative restrictions (Article XI) were reaffirmed. The TRIMs introduced 'standstill' and 'rollback' mechanisms applicable only to local content rules, trade balancing and foreign exchange balancing. Export performance requirements were not dealt with since several developed and developing countries have been using investment incentives and performance requirements.

A committee was set up as per the agreement to monitor the implementation of TRIMs commitments. The member-countries were given 90 days to notify the WTO of any existing TRIMs. Further, member-countries were granted a transition period during which their notified TRIMs were to be eliminated. The duration of transition period was based on the level of development — developed countries were given two years; developing countries five years; and the least-developed countries were granted seven years. Article 5.3 of the Agreement allows the developing and the least-developed countries to apply for an extension of the transition period. Several member-countries (for instance, Argentina, Chile, Malaysia and Pakistan) have submitted requests for extension of the transition period. However, under accession protocols, countries are required to comply with the TRIMs on accession without any transition period. For instance, China gave specific commitments to foreign investors without any transition period.

In the TRIMs agreement, there are some exemptions for the developing countries, who can deviate temporarily on account of balance-of-payments problems. The disputes under TRIMs are subject to the same settlement mechanism as other disputes governed by the Dispute Settlement Understanding of the WTO. Some developing countries (for instance, Brazil and India) are demanding substantial reduction in the scope of TRIMs agreement so that it gives them flexibility to use performance requirements to promote technology transfer and domestic industrialization.

2. General Agreement on Trade in Services (GATS): This is the first multilateral, legally enforceable agreement that covers trade and investment in services. The GATS encompasses over 160 service activities including banking, telecommunication, energy, and education. The GATS outlines the obligations for trade in services in a similar manner that the GATT earmarked for trade in goods. The GATS is aimed at eliminating governmental measures that prevent services from being freely traded across national borders or that discriminate against locally established service firms with foreign ownership. It incorporates the "right of establishment," under which service providers have the right to enter another market by establishing commercial presence in sectors where countries have made specific commitments. Critics have rightly pointed out that GATS is an indirect way of introducing an agreement on investment, since one of the modes of trade in services is commercial presence. Commitments under commercial presence imply not only opening up of commercial services (such as banking and insurance) to foreign investment but, more significantly, vital social services like health and education.

Under the GATS, the three important principles are MFN treatment, market access and national treatment. MFN treatment means a country has to treat the service supplier of another member-country no less favorably than it does the service supplier of any other member-country of the WTO. Market access obligations imply that a country is bound to allow foreign service suppliers to enter its market for providing services. National treatment refers to treating foreign suppliers under the same terms and conditions laid out for domestic suppliers.

The GATS employs a unique approach under which some obligations (such as MFN) are applied to all service sectors unless specifically exempted, while some others (national treatment and market access) are not applicable to service sectors unless specifically included in the "schedules of commitments" notified by the member-country. The countries are bound to liberalize only those sectors for which they have provided schedules and to the extent of the commitments undertaken in those schedules. This process is called 'positive listing' or 'bottom-up' approach. In contrast, 'negative listing' or 'top-down' approach implies that the obligations apply to all sectors unless a country specifically lists an exception. The oft-repeated claims that GATS-type approach is flexible and development-friendly require fresh thinking in the light of GATS 2000 negotiations. Given the unequal power relations, developing countries have been compelled to undertake greater commitments over time by narrowing down the flexibility available to them. For instance, the EU request list seeks removal of a wide range of regulatory measures in several sectors (e.g., telecommunications, environmental and financial services) which developing countries had listed in the last round.

Since service sector is subject to tight regulatory measures, the GATS became a part of WTO only after a protracted negotiating process. Though many countries were initially keen to keep the GATS outside the purview of the WTO, the negotiators were able to bring it under the WTO. All members of the WTO are signatories to the GATS framework and have made different commitments for different service sectors. A new round of service sector negotiations was mandated for the year 2000 and every five years thereafter. Since the biggest exporters of services are the US and

EU, they are expanding the scope of GATS through progressive rounds of negotiations. The developing countries, on the other hand, are advocating inclusion of safeguard provisions in the GATS to ensure that global service providers do not pose a threat to domestic entities.

At the end of the Uruguay Round, the GATS called for extended negotiations in four service sectors: basic telecommunications, financial services, movement of natural persons, and maritime transport services. Negotiations for the first two sectors were concluded in 1997. Negotiations on movement of natural persons were finalized in 1995, though negotiations on maritime transport were suspended. The Financial Services Agreement (FSA) came into force in March 1999. By covering financial services including banking, securities and insurance, the FSA marked a major departure from the past as member-countries had agreed to a legal framework for cross-border trade, market access and dispute settlement mechanism. It has been estimated that the FSA covers nearly 95 per cent of global trade in banking, insurance, securities and other financial services. Although several countries have not undertaken comprehensive reforms as envisaged under the FSA, yet the developed countries, particularly the US, have used the agreement to open up the financial sector in the developing countries and emerging markets.

The dispute settlement mechanism of the WTO deals with any violation of commitments by the member-countries. Under the dispute settlement mechanism, a country may be required to give compensation if the tribunal finds that the member-country has not adhered to its commitments and is not making the necessary changes in policies.

In addition to TRIMS and GATS, the Trade-Related Aspects of

Intellectual Property Rights (TRIPs) agreement also has provisions for liberalizing investment policies as it incorporates protection of intellectual property (patents and copyright) — a form of intangible asset. Besides, there are other less known WTO agreements (such as anti-dumping agreement, agreement on subsidies and countervailing measures, and agreement on government procurement) which also cover investment issues.

Do Investment Agreements Lead to Increased Foreign Investments?

Embedded in neoliberalism, current approaches advocating global investment rules are based on several false notions which need to be debunked. Does signing of investment agreements necessarily lead to a spurt in foreign investment? There is no empirical evidence to prove conclusively that investment agreements lead to increased foreign investments. Nor do they boost the prospects of obtaining investments in future. If the African experience is any guide, investment agreements *per se* cannot increase the quantum of foreign investment, leave aside the quality of foreign investment.

Based on past experiences with bilateral investment agreements, researchers have come to the conclusion that there is no causal relationship between bilateral investment agreements and increased foreign investment. In a comprehensive study, Mary Hallward-Driemeier of the World Bank, found that bilateral investment agreements had no singular impact on increasing investment to developing countries.[7] Studies undertaken by UNCTAD have also revealed that there is little correlation between receiving increased foreign investment and signing of bilateral investment agreements.[8] On the contrary, there are ample cases where substantial foreign investments have taken place in several developing countries in the absence of bilateral investment agreements. This is well-illustrated by substantial US investment in China.

Since the 1980s, a large number of developing countries have signed numerous bilateral investment agreements, yet they receive less than one-third of total FDI flows. Further, FDI flows are highly concentrated in a few developing countries. Bulk of FDI flows have gone to a few developing countries like China, Brazil, Mexico and Argentina. In 2001, only five countries accounted for 62 per cent of the total FDI flows to the developing world.[9] While 49 least developed countries (LDCs) received only 2 per cent of total FDI flows to the developing world and 0.5 per cent of world FDI.[10] Similarly, bulk of portfolio investment flows are concentrated in a few 'emerging markets' of Latin America and Asia.

A closer look at investment trends in Africa confirms that investment agreements do not guarantee increased investment. According to UNCTAD, 53 African countries have concluded 533 investment agreements (an average of 10 per country) by the end of 2002.[11] In addition, they have liberalized regulatory regimes and carried out large-scale privatization of public enterprises and financial reforms in the last two decades. Yet Africa receives less than 2 per cent of the total FDI flows. Aimed at exploiting natural resources, bulk of FDI flows are concentrated in a few countries such as Nigeria, Angola, Botswana, Ghana and Algeria.

It is disturbing to note that FDI flows to Africa are actually declining with the signing of new investment agreements. For instance, FDI flows declined from $19 billion in 2001 to $11 billion in 2002 despite 78 new investment agreements signed by the African countries. It is not lack of investment agreements that prevent the flow of foreign investment to Africa, rather small size of domestic markets, poor infrastructure, locational disadvantages, unskilled labor, civil unrest and political instability in the continent which are responsible for meager inflows.

If bilateral agreements, which are considered to be lopsided, unbalanced and dictated by rich countries to serve the interests of their investors, have so far failed to increase foreign investment, it stands to reason that a 'balanced' multilateral investment agreement in the WTO is unlikely to boost foreign investment in the developing countries.

Benefits of Global Investment Rules: Myths and Realities

The proponents of global investment rules have failed to produce substantial evidence in support of their arguments, as is evident from the debates in *Financial Times*.[12] A common perception that multilateral investment rules would bring an end to bilateral agreements is flawed on two counts. First, adoption of a multilateral investment agreement would not necessarily imply an end to bilateral agreements. Notwithstanding the establishment of a multilateral trade regime under WTO, the US and European Union have initiated and concluded several bilateral and regional trade agreements in recent years. Nearly 300 such agreements have been signed and notified to the WTO. Significantly, the bilateral free trade agreements signed by the US with Jordan, Chile and Singapore include aggressive safeguards for intellectual property rights, which go well beyond the benchmarks set in the WTO's trade-related aspects of intellectual property rights (TRIPS) agreement. The treaties with Chile and Singapore also include strict financial conditions curbing the use of capital controls. Under these provisions, in case Chile and Singapore impose capital controls to defend their economies, they would end up compensating American investors.

If these experiences are any indicator, it would be incorrect to infer that once a multilateral investment agreement comes into force, the world would be free of a plethora of existing bilateral and regional investment agreements. With developed countries and corporate lobby groups such as the International Chamber of Commerce consistently seeking higher standards of market access and investment protection, there is no guarantee that a multilateral agreement would put a stop to investment agreements in future. On the contrary, a multilateral agreement would act as the 'floor' for working out comprehensive bilateral and regional investment agreements in future.

Second, the argument that a multilateral investment agreement is preferable because it would enhance the bargaining power of weak countries betrays a lack of basic understanding about politics and power relations. It would be too simplistic to assume that unequal power relations only exist at the bilateral level. Unequal power relations are manifested at every level, be it bilateral, regional or multilateral.

Proponents also claim that the purpose of global investment rules is to promote transparency in the host countries.[13] If promoting transparency is the real objective, why create complex binding rules pertaining to national treatment, performance requirements, expropriation and dispute settlement mechanisms that could restrict governments' ability to regulate foreign investment. Transparency can be better promoted through much simpler mechanisms and on a best endeavor basis. One is not arguing that investment policies of countries should not be transparent, but should not the same principles be applicable to foreign investors as well? The issue acquires greater significance since transnational corporations have become the dominant players in the contemporary world economy with little public accountability. Recent corporate scandals, from Enron to WorldCom, have highlighted the need for greater corporate transparency, disclosures and accountability.

Ironically, proponents of multilateral investment rules while demanding transparency of state institutions vehemently oppose attempts to enforce similar obligations on foreign investors.

It is also difficult to accept the contention that transparency is the crucial component that influences decisions of foreign investors to invest. If lack of transparency is the root cause hindering investment, China's ability to attract $53 billion of foreign investment in 2002 needs to be explained. That China has been able to corner investments of such magnitude without any semblance of transparency adopted in most democratically governed regimes is a pointer to the fact that there is no causal relationship between extent of transparency and investment flows. The same is the case with Central and Eastern Europe that witnessed a surfeit of foreign investment in its banking sector in the 1990s without adhering to any transparency and disclosure standards. Moreover, it is highly debatable whether WTO is the proper forum to inculcate transparency, as its decision-making processes do not pay heed to the principles of transparency and democratic accountability. As witnessed in the Doha conference, draft Ministerial Text was made available to member-countries at the eleventh hour which hardly left any time for wider consultations.

Another myth propagated by the advocates of investment rules is that such rules would help in creating level-playing field. But the reality is completely opposite. Already the playing field is tilted against the domestic businesses of the developing countries. By providing greater market access and protection to foreign investors, playing fields would get further skewed in favor of giant TNCs.

Some proponents have even argued that global investment rules would be more beneficial to small and medium-sized enterprises (SMEs).[14] It needs to be recognized that majority of

SMEs (in both developed and developing countries) are essentially catering to domestic markets. Only a miniscule of SMEs has the economic clout or inclination to invest overseas. For the rest, the real challenge is to maintain their hold on the domestic markets in the wake of greater competition posed by transnational firms. Besides, the experience of investment liberalization has not been positive for SMEs, irrespective of their location. Capital mobility facilitated by investment rules could further harm the interests of the SMEs. In fact, the giant transnational corporations would be the real beneficiaries of investment rules.

The widespread notion that since trade and investment are closely linked, they should be dealt by a single organization (i.e., WTO) also lacks conviction. Given this logic, there is no need for International Labor Organization and International Monetary Fund because trade issues are also closely linked with labor and finance issues. Should these institutions be closed down and their mandate handed over to the WTO?

FDI is not a Panacea

Since the hard selling of global investment rules is based on much-touted benefits of FDI, it becomes imperative to examine the linkages between FDI and economic growth. Advocates of investment rules take it for granted that FDI offers immense benefits to countries in terms of transfer of technology, creation of jobs, expanding exports, easing balance of payment constraints, providing quality products and services along with managerial efficiency. The perceived benefits may hold true for some FDI, but it would be a serious mistake to make broad generalizations based on such investments.

There is hardly any reliable cross-country empirical evidence to support the claim that FDI *per se* accelerates economic growth.

Box 2.1

Cross-Border M&A Mania

Since the 1990s, TNCs are widely using the strategy of mergers and acquisitions (M&As) to consolidate and expand their global reach. Instead of launching 'greenfield' investments and projects which create new opportunities for employment and competition, TNCs rather prefer the easy route of M&A to consolidate their economic power. In reality, M&A add little to productive capacity but are simply transfer of ownership and control with no change in the actual asset base. The major negative fallout of M&A activity is the promotion of monopolistic tendencies, which in turn, curb competition and widen the scope for price manipulations. In situations where M&A deals are not possible because of anti-competition regulations, TNCs often form commercial alliances, as evident in the case of airline industry.

After acquisition, corporations often break up the newly acquired firms, reduce workforce and indulge in various malpractices to curb competition. Therefore, M&As have become one of the quickest means to acquire new markets. These deals generally lead to strategic firms and sectors of economy (e.g., infrastructure and banking) coming under the total control of TNCs. As top managements carry out M&A deals with the primary objective of raising shareholder value (rather than making strategic gains), it is not surprising that M&A deals have markedly flourished in the bullish financial markets.

At the global level, cross-border M&As account for the bulk of FDI flows. Due to M&A, the landscape of global corporate world is not only rapidly changing but also becoming more and more complex. A look at the top global 500 TNCs list over the past few years reveals that several well-known corporations have either disappeared or merged into a new entity. As a result, the list of top global 500 TNCs keeps changing every year. In the year 2000, Exxon Mobil, Citigroup, DaimlerChrysler, JP Morgan Chase & Co. secured top positions in the top 500 list of TNCs only due to M&A.

contd. on next page

The year 2000 was an important milestone in the history of global M&A deals. It witnessed record M&A deals both in terms of numbers and value. There were as many as 38292 M&A deals, totaling nearly $3500 billion in the year 2000. Interestingly, more than half of M&A deals took place in US confirming that M&A mania had gripped corporate America. The bulk of M&A activity at the international level is taking place in the financial and banking sectors.

Since the first half of 2001, M&A deals have gone down dramatically. There are several reasons behind this decline. Firstly, there has been an exceptional fall in the share prices globally, especially with the bursting of high-tech bubble. Secondly, the specter of global economic slowdown, particularly in the US, is fast becoming a reality. Lastly, the adverse results and experiences of several previous M&A deals have come to light. On paper, mergers and acquisitions sound attractive but in the real world, synergies often do not materialize. Since each corporation has a distinct work culture, it becomes an uphill task for the board, management and workers to function cohesively in the aftermath of a M&A deal.

Most of M&A deals have not yielded desired results. Despite the massive layoff of workers and organizational restructuring, two-thirds of M&As have failed to achieve the intended objectives. Several instances (e.g., DaimlerChrysler) have come to light where corporations suffered huge losses after M&A. The *Businessweek's* report, "The Merger Hangover," found that 61 per cent of mergers between 1995 and 2001 destroyed shareholder wealth. This puts a big question mark on the real objective of M&A deals.

In the present circumstances, it is quite difficult to establish direct linkages between FDI and economic growth if other factors such as competition policy, labor skills, physical infrastructure, policy interventions, macroeconomic management, regulatory framework and political stability are not taken into account. Further, in the absence of performance requirements and other regulations, many of the stated benefits of FDI would not occur. ·

The positive impact of FDI depends on several factors including the sector in which the investment is taking place. For instance, if the bulk of FDI flows are directed towards exploitation of natural resources in the host countries (as in the case of Africa), then the benefits in terms of transfer of technology, knowledge and skills would be negligible.

Nowadays majority of FDI flows are nowadays associated with cross-border mergers and acquisitions rather than greenfield investments — the establishment of new industrial and service units. As a result, their positive impact on the domestic economy through technological transfers and other spillover effects has been significantly diluted (see Box 2.1).

Another guiding principle that determines the impact of FDI on national economic growth is whether foreign investment complements or substitutes domestic investment. In several developing countries, it has been observed that foreign investment often crowds out domestic investment. This phenomenon is more evident in Latin America where cross-border mergers and acquisitions are the dominant form of FDI inflows.

Many commentators favor FDI over other forms of capital flows as it does not involve repayment of debt and interest. It is true that FDI does not involve direct repayment of debt and interest but substantial foreign exchange outflows could take place on account of remittance of profits, dividends, royalty payments, technical fees and import of raw materials and technology. Substantial foreign exchange outflows could also take place due to manipulative transfer pricing by TNCs.

No doubt, FDI related to exports could generate foreign exchange but investments in non-tradable sectors (such as telecommunications, power, retail, water and sanitation) could involve substantial foreign exchange outflows in various forms, thereby augmenting balance of payments problems in host countries.

Furthermore, the other attributes of FDI flows have also changed profoundly over the years. The traditional distinctions between FDI and other capital flows are getting increasingly blurred. FDI is no longer as stable as it used to be in the past. The stability of FDI has been questioned in the light of growing evidence which suggests that as a financial crisis becomes imminent, transnational corporations indulge in hedging activities to cover their exchange rate risk which, in turn, generates additional pressure on the currencies.

The claim that TNCs offer international quality products and create employment in host countries may not always hold true. There are ample examples (for instance, bottled water in India) where transnational corporations have not followed international quality standards in providing goods and services. Since FDI is usually concentrated in capital-intensive industries, the creation of employment opportunities is largely limited to highly skilled workers. Thus, it would be erroneous to assume that FDI can solve the problem of large-scale unemployment in the poor and the developing world.

The predatory business practices of TNCs and their adverse consequences on the domestic businesses, particularly infant industries, are well documented and therefore need no elaboration here. Foreign investment in resources extraction activities such as mining could involve large-scale displacement of people and environmental hazards. Traditional economic indicators have failed to

measure the exact social and environmental costs of such investment. Several instances have been reported suggesting that investors are relocating their polluting industries from the developed
countries to countries with lower environmental standards. Although lower environmental standards in the developing countries
may not be the primary reason for relocation, a study conducted by
the author found that several German investors were influenced by
it while relocating their dye industry in India.[15]

Given the fact that there is no country (large or small, developed or developing) which has achieved rapid economic growth
and development by solely relying on FDI, it is time that the stated
benefits of FDI need to be reconsidered. What is good for TNCs
may not be good for the host countries.

Is WTO an Appropriate Forum for Investment Rules?

Given the fact that trade related investment issues have already
been covered under TRIMs agreement, there is no justification for
establishing comprehensive investment rules at the WTO. This
raises an important question whether the WTO is an appropriate
venue for negotiating an agreement on investment. Elizabeth Smythe
examined this issue in the context of addressing the basic question
of why some countries choose particular international organizations as their preferred venue for negotiations on international
investment rules.[16] She concluded that countries' own investment
interests drive their preferences for a particular venue. According
to Smythe, countries view international economic organizations
strategically and their influence within these organizations shapes
their decisions about where negotiations should take place.[17] For
instance, EU prefers the WTO for investment negotiations due to
the fact that it could bargain as a united front at the WTO against
countries like the US.[18]

The establishment of investment rules in the WTO would open a Pandora's box. With emphasis on enlarging and protecting foreign investors' rights, investment rules could constrict the policy space of countries to maneuver investment policies in accordance with their developmental priorities. Although the EU and some other developed countries favor the adoption of a GATS-type approach on investment agreement in the WTO allowing countries to select sectors which they wish to liberalize, there is no guarantee that it would provide adequate policy space to member-countries. By 'locking in' reforms, the GATS approach generates additional pressure on countries to undertake wider commitments over the years. It is pertinent to point out that once a country gives market access commitments in the WTO, it becomes difficult to reverse it if not impossible. Likewise, an agreement covering many but not all developing countries would also be problematic, as it would in effect compel outsiders to join later on.

Further, it is difficult to fathom the relationship between a prospective investment agreement at the WTO and the existence of over 1800 bilateral and regional investment treaties. What would be the fate of these agreements if a multilateral agreement at the WTO comes into force? Would existing investment agreements become null and void? Till now, the Working Group on Trade and Investment at the WTO has not contemplated on this important aspect.

The mandate of WTO is confined to trade in goods and services. It has neither the jurisdiction nor the competence to deal with comprehensive investment rules. For instance, WTO trade arbitrators lack the expertise to assess the quantum of compensation to be awarded to a foreign investor in the eventuality of violation of the terms of proposed agreement by a member-country. Further, inclusion of investor-state dispute settlement provisions in a prospective investment framework (as demanded by several

Box 2.2

Are Corporate Codes of Conduct the Solution?

Of late, sections of NGOs, trade unions and anti-corporate movements have evinced keen interest on corporate code of conduct and self-regulation. In fact, several environmental and human rights NGOs have played a key role in drafting codes of conduct for TNCs.

Over the years, a variety of such codes have been formulated in response to growing awareness among consumers in the developed countries. The list includes International Labor Organization's Tripartite Declaration of Principles Concerning Multinational Enterprises and Social Policy; the OECD Guidelines on Multinational Enterprises; the UNCTAD Set of Multilaterally Agreed Equitable Principles and Rules for the Control of Restrictive Business Practices; the Food and Agriculture Organization's Code on the Distribution and Use of Pesticides; the World Health Organization and UNICEF Code of Marketing Breast Milk Substitutes, etc. Corporations have also adopted similar codes such as the US Chemical Manufacturers Association's Responsible Care Program and the International Chamber of Commerce's Business Charter for Sustainable Development.

In operation for several years, corporate codes of conduct remain weak and ineffective because they are voluntary, non-binding agreements. Moreover, corporate codes are limited to a few sectors, particularly those where brand names play a decisive role such as garments, footwear, toys, sport goods, consumer goods and retailing businesses. But the major sectors of economy remain outside the purview of corporate codes. Usually, codes are not universally binding on all operations of the company including contractors, subsidiaries, suppliers and agents. Further, many codes do not entail the right to organize, form unions and collective bargaining. Without such basic rights, codes remain ineffective.

contd. on next page

Another problematic issue pertains to the actual implementation and monitoring of voluntary codes. Compliance with codes of conduct is voluntary. No government can enforce them. In other words, codes do not involve any penalties on TNCs who violate them. Numerous cases could be cited where the corporations are signatories to the voluntary standards but refuse to comply with them.

Since big consultancy firms usually carry out monitoring of codes with little transparency and public participation, the actual implementation of codes by TNCs remain a closely guarded secret. This strengthens the suspicion that voluntary codes are meant to deflect public criticism rather than tackling the ground conditions. The mushrooming of voluntary codes in an era of increasingly deregulated business and trade raises doubts about their efficacy. Unlike the 1970s when codes of conduct for TNCs were largely pushed by the developing countries, it is mainly the developed countries who have been vigorously promoting the voluntary codes since the 1990s. Therefore, it is not surprising that there is a propensity among the advocates of neoliberalism to consider voluntary codes of conduct as a substitute to state regulations.

The voluntary codes of conduct can never be a substitute for state regulations. Nor can they substitute labor and community rights. At best, voluntary codes can complement state regulations and provide space for raising environmental, health, labor and other issues.

If the recent experience is any guide, the struggle for implementation of voluntary codes could be a frustrating, time-consuming exercise. It dissipates the enthusiasm for launching struggle for regulatory controls on TNCs. This was evident in the case of the decade-long campaign on the national code and law for promoting breast-feeding and restricting the marketing of baby food by the TNCs in India. Therefore, voluntary codes require serious rethinking on the part of those who consider these as a cure-all to problems posed by the transnational capital.

corporate lobby groups) could entail fundamental changes in the WTO's structure since it is essentially an inter-state agency.

Another problematic issue pertains to the liberalization of capital account. At present, balance-of-payment issues in the WTO are restricted to current account transactions. But investment rules at the WTO would necessitate liberalization of capital account by member-countries. In the aftermath of Southeast Asian financial crisis, there has been a rethinking on liberalization of capital account as it emasculates the ability of developing countries to protect themselves from the whims of volatile capital flows. The contention that developing countries would become more vulnerable to volatile capital flows under a prospective investment agreement at the WTO cannot be overlooked.

It is also unrealistic to assume that an investment agreement in the WTO could be formulated that would take into account development concerns and diverse interests of its 148 member-countries. The collapse of negotiations on MAI at the OECD (a relatively homogeneous grouping of 29 countries with highly liberalized investment regimes) in the 1998 has amply demonstrated that one-size-fits-all strategy on investment is off the mark. The one-size-fits-all strategy on investment is ill conceived because WTO members are at different stages of development. What is good for capital-exporting Japan may not be good for capital-importing Bangladesh.

Investment Rules for Whom?

The advocates of investment rules in the WTO have paid little attention on restrictions to be imposed on predatory business practices, manipulative transfer pricing, anti-labor policies, bribery and other corrupt practices employed by foreign investors. Particularly in the light of corporate scandals (from Enron to Parmalat), the issue of investor responsibilities cannot be overlooked. Despite much-touted claims of corporate transparency and disclosures, the basic norms of governance were completely flouted by these mega corporations. Regulations related to accounting and reporting were either circumvented or followed in letter rather than in spirit. What is even more disturbing is the fact that most of these corporations used to have their own codes of conduct. Although it is a different matter that these corporations violated their own codes. These scandals have exposed the systemic flaws of highly acclaimed American corporate governance model based on self-regulation. Hence, voluntary codes of conduct are insufficient to ensure that TNCs would conduct their business operations responsibly and therefore should not be regarded as a substitute for state regulations (see Box 2.2).

Concluding Remarks

Since diverse forms of legal and administrative rules governing foreign investment at the national level thwart the smooth operation of transnational capital, investment rules with stringent provisions on foreign investment liberalization and protection have become imperative in the emergent world economic order. The overarching objective of global investment rules is to weaken the regulatory capacity of governments to ensure that they remain subservient to the interests of foreign capital. It is in this context that the rationale behind a multilateral investment agreement in the WTO needs to be examined and contested.

Notes and References

1. Ha-Joon Chang, *Kicking Away the Ladder: Development Strategy in Historical Perspective*, Anthem Press, London, 2002.

2. Francisco Sercovich, "Best Practices, Policy Convergence, and the WTO Trade-related Investment Measures,"*Cepal Review*, No. 64, 1998, pp. 93-112.

3. Gary Pursell, "The Australian Experience with FDI and Local Content Programmes in the Auto Industry," paper presented at the conference on WTO, Technology Transfer and Globalisation of Firms, Institute of Economic Growth, New Delhi, March 1999, (mimeo).

4. For a detailed analysis of Pepsico's commitments in India, see Kavaljit Singh, *Broken Commitments: The Case of Pepsi in India*, PIRG Update, No. 1, New Delhi, June 1997.

5. For details, see Kavaljit Singh, *Multilateral Investment Agreement in the WTO: Issues and Illusions*, Policy Paper No. 1, Asia-Pacific Research Network, Manila, 2003.

6. Jurgen Kurtz, "A General Investment Agreement in the WTO?: Lessons from Chapter 11 of NAFTA and the OECD Multilateral Agreement on Investment," *Jean Monnet Working Paper 6/02*, New York University School of Law, New York, 2002.

7. Mary Hallward-Driemeier, "Bilateral Investment Treaties: Do They Increase FDI Flows?," Background Paper for *Global Economic Prospects 2003: Investing to Unlock Global Opportunities*, World Bank, Washington D.C., 2002.

8. UNCTAD, *Bilateral Investment Treaties in the mid-1990s*, United Nations, New York, 1998.

9. UNCTAD, *World Investment Report 2002*, United Nations, New York and Geneva, 2002, p. 9.

10. Ibid.

11. UNCTAD, *World Investment Report 2003*, United Nations, New York and Geneva, 2003, p. 36.

12. My article, "Keep Investment Pacts off Cancun's Agenda," *Financial Times*, July 7, 2003, evoked several responses from the proponents of global investment rules. In particular, see Maria Livanos Cattaui, "Multilateral Investment Pacts Should be on Cancun Agenda," *Financial Times*, July 9, 2003; and Kerstin Berglof, "Multilateral Investment Agreements will not Hurt Developing Countries," *Financial Times*, July 28, 2003.

13. Kerstin Berglof, op. cit.

14. Noboru Hatakeyama, "The World Needs Investment Rules," *Financial Times*, August 1, 2003.

15. Kavaljit Singh, *The Reality of Foreign Investment: German Investments in India (1991-96)*, Madhyam Books, New Delhi, 1996.

16. Elizabeth Smythe, "Your Place or Mine?: States, International Organization and the Negotiation on Investment Rules," *Transnational Corporations*, Volume 7, No. 3, December 1998, pp. 85-120.

17. Ibid., p. 113.

18. Ibid., p. 114.

CHAPTER 3

Does Globalization Promote Democracy and Human Rights?

We wanted democracy, but we ended up with the bond market.

Polish graffiti

THERE is a strong tendency among hyper-globalists to view globalization and democracy as compatible and complementary phenomena. In reality, globalization and democracy involve several complex and paradoxical processes that operate and intersect unevenly at various levels. Like globalization, democracy is not amenable to precise definition. Democracy may imply different things to different people who have very little in common in terms of their worldview, ideology and class status. From leaders of labor unions to the captains of transnational capital, from anti-corporate popular movements to powerful states and multilateral institutions — all swear by democracy. The grounds for supporting democracy are as diverse as their avowed proponents.

Notwithstanding popular acceptance of democracy at the global level, the discourse on democracy is increasingly becoming superficial and constricted. Most analysts tend to equate democracy with the notion of political democracy valorizing the right of franchise and free elections. Without belittling the values of political democracy such as the right to vote, free and fair elections, and freedom to form associations, the fact remains that such a narrow approach cannot help in understanding the myriad issues related to the democratic processes of decision-making in social life. Viewed in totality, the notion of democracy encompasses rule of law; freedom of speech; freedom to form associations; enjoyment of basic economic, social and political rights by all citizens; equitable distribution of wealth, income and resources; restraining privileges of elites; the right to dissent; the right to choose alternatives; and safeguarding the rights of minorities as an abiding faith of pluralism.

Contrary to popular perception, democracy is not an end in itself. It is an evolving process and has the potential to become a potent instrument for radical transformation provided it is applied in all spheres of social life. Democracy cannot be implanted or imposed, it has to be imbibed and nourished from within. That is why, there is no universal model of democracy. The democratic processes vary from country to country because societies differ in terms of history, culture and popular aspirations. Switzerland, for instance, developed a decentralized, confederate system rooted in self-governance of 'cantons,' while UK evolved a centralized system based on representative parliamentary democracy. Democracy in France emerged under the influence of the church whereas India developed parliamentary democratic system based on the Westminster model with a strong emphasis on secularism.

Experience of democracy promotion in several nascent democracies reveals that democratization cannot be achieved through technical approaches aimed at replicating the western model of liberal democracy or through technical kits such as training of parliamentarians, civil servants and judges. Democratization would remain elusive until and unless, there is a political will among the country's political leadership and people at large. The top-down

Box 3.1

Globalization and Democracy:
Two Sides of the Same Coin?

The common usage of terms associated with globalization process such as 'free market,' 'liberalization' and 'openness' is often perceived as synonymous to democratization. There is no linear connection between globalization and democracy. Democracy cannot be attained merely through unbridled privatization, deregulation and free movement of goods and capital across borders. Nor can it be achieved by acquisition of jeans, colas, burgers, pop music and computers. Primarily because globalization thrives on passive consumers while democracy is sustained by active participation of citizens. For globalization, consumers call the shots while democracy without active citizens is meaningless.

Globalization may provide a plethora of luxury cars to the rich and affluent classes but a public transportation system cannot be built by putting more and more cars on the roads. In the same vein, a sound public health care system cannot be developed by merely procuring expensive patented drugs and state-of-the-art private hospitals. A public sanitation system is much more than the flooding the markets with aromatic toiletries. Overflowing shopping malls and superstores can satiate endless appetite of the affluent classes for consumer goods but can these fulfill the basic needs of poor masses who lack purchasing power?

Globalization may provide unlimited opportunities to international fund managers and their local counterparts to indulge in speculative activities in financial markets but it constrains the scope of pro-poor and redistributive policies. The rights of the minuscule international investors and fund managers cannot be equated with the rights of the poor citizens. Freedom does not merely imply the freedom to accumulate property and wealth, and justice denotes much more than the protection of property rights.

technical approach remains ignorant of the fact that democratization is essentially a political process which can only be addressed by domestic popular movements. Without taking into account the underlying power relations and socio-economic matrix, technical approaches by themselves are hardly adequate for the realization of democracy.

Globalization of Democracy

The last two decades have witnessed a discernible shift in the political systems of several countries. Political liberalization has accompanied economic liberalization in most parts of the world. Authoritarian political regimes, which held sway during 1950-80 in Latin America, Africa and Asia, have given way to democratic regimes based on multiparty system and periodic elections. A majority of these regimes have granted varying degrees of political rights and individual freedom to their citizens. In fact, over 160 out of a total of 185 countries are nowadays governed by 'democratic' regimes. Whereas some countries (e.g., China, Vietnam, North Korea and Cuba) are still being governed by communist regimes. Democracy being the rule, electoral activity around the world has also witnessed a boom. During 1990-99, there were 300 competitive elections in democratic countries.[1]

In the new global setting, bloody power struggles and military coups have become anathema to the world. Even dictators (for instance, General Pervez Musharraf in Pakistan) are holding referendums and elections to gain democratic legitimacy in the eyes of their own people and the world community. In some countries, army generals are running for power in multi-party elections (for instance, Presidential elections in Nigeria in 2003). Such a sudden transformation of political regimes within a span of two decades has been unprecedented in the annals of history. Free and regular elections, freedom of expression, freedom of association, and mush-rooming of civil society organizations were unthinkable in countries under authoritarian rule till recently. Hence, the real value of such achievements for those people, who had struggled and suffered during the authoritarian reign, needs to be acknowledged.

Nonetheless, the transition to formal democratic regimes has not been smooth in many countries. In several nascent democracies, from Haiti to Fiji, spread of democracy has proved elusive. Ironically, in those countries (for instance, Indonesia) where political democracy has taken roots, rampant corruption, abuse of power and ethnic conflicts have given a setback to popular aspirations. As a result, initial euphoria associated with the project of democracy promotion soon evaporated. The traditional distinctions between democratic and authoritarian regimes are getting blurred and the world is witnessing a whole range of political systems from illiberal democracies to covert authoritarian structures.

A host of external and internal factors paved the way for most authoritarian regimes to accept formal democracy. Among the external factors, the end of Cold War coupled with the pressure exerted by the powerful states and multilateral institutions were the most important ones. With the waning of the specter of communism, dictators in several Latin American and Asian countries are no longer getting the kind of financial, military and political support from the US and other powerful states that they used to. The notable exception is General Pervez Musharraf regime in Pakistan. Indeed, the US support to Musharraf regime had more to do with geo-political exigencies as Pakistan's airspace and logistical support was desperately required in the war against the Taliban regime in Afganistan.

By linking democracy as a condition for development aid, the international donor agencies have also played an important role in democracy promotion. Bilateral aid agencies, in particular the US Agency for International Development (USAID), the British Department for International Development (DFID) and the Swedish International Development Cooperation Agency (SIDA), spend millions of dollars each year to support democracy programs in several third world countries. The UN and its agencies have also been active in promoting democracy in those countries ravaged by civil war and ethnic conflicts such as Kosovo, Sudan and East Timor. In addition, regional groupings such as EU have adopted democracy as a necessary precondition for membership. Private foundations are also not far behind. For instance, the Open Society, founded by George Soros, spent more than $120 million in promoting democracy projects in Central and Eastern Europe between 1989 and 1994.

Another major factor behind the spread of democracy is the discrediting of authoritarian regimes in many parts of the world despite the fact that rapid economic growth was achieved under some regimes. The authoritarian regimes not only got discredited in the eyes of their own people, but even the foreign investors, for whom political stability is a prerequisite for investment, no longer endorse dictators. The reasons are obvious. Past experiences with the authoritarian regimes in several countries such as Philippines, Chile and Zaire show that these regimes have been unable to cope with the threats posed against the interests of transnational elites by mass movements seeking democratization of social life.

International powers have realized that earlier mechanisms of domination have failed to ensure social control and stability. The consequences of direct invasion or military coup by dictators had been catastrophic. Political regimes installed through such coercive means were responsible for chronic instability and economic ruin.

Besides, the blatant use of force has engendered mass movements that not only desire removal of authoritarian regimes but, more importantly, seek radical democratization of power and equitable distribution of wealth and income. Emergence of such mass movements on a world scale has the potentiality to seriously endanger the globalization project and thereby the interests of global and local elites. In such a scenario, a formal multi-party democratic regime is considered more reliable because it can ensure internal political stability and smooth transfer of power.

The Political Project of Globalization

Neoliberal globalization is not only an economic project but also has a political component. The economic project of neoliberal globalization is based on free movement of goods and capital while the political project is aimed at globalizing national political and legal processes. Diverse forms of legal, administrative and political systems act as an impediment in the smooth functioning of a global market economy. That is why, various international institutions like the World Bank, IMF and WTO have stepped in to create a uniform political, administrative and legal system at the global level in order to ensure smooth operation of transnational capital. Promotion of democracy has, therefore, become an integral part of the emergent global economic order.

As discussed in the next chapter, political and institutional reforms have been imposed as a necessary precondition for economic integration by IFIs. Since markets do not function in a vacuum, a rule based legal regime is necessary for the smooth functioning of markets. Legal and institutional reforms are oriented towards securing private property rights, enforcing contracts and expansion of private sector. The new emphasis on 'sound economic management' may appear a laudable goal but is nothing

Kavaljit Singh

more than a rigid adherence to fiscal austerity measures. Even the limited concerns for safety nets are attempts to contain mass uprisings against the neoliberal economic order rather than making people economically independent and empowered. Thus, governance reforms are biased towards strengthening market economy instead of genuine democratization and attainment of human rights.

Over the years, 'Good Governance' has become both as an objective and a precondition for development aid. Nowadays it is difficult to come across aid packages of multilateral financial institutions and bilateral donors that do not use the term 'good governance' and contain governance conditionalities. The present governance reforms agenda lacks coherence and consistency and therefore needs to be questioned. There is strong tendency among the international aid community to equate governance within the ambit of state institutions and structures with an emphasis on corruption, transparency, participation and rule of law. Without belittling the importance of these measures, the fact remains that such a narrow approach cannot help in understanding the myriad issues related to the concept of good governance. A good governance system is the one under which all public policy affairs are managed through broad consensus in a transparent, accountable, participatory and equitable manner. Viewed in totality, the notion of governance would encompass all non-state actors particularly markets and civil society.

The good governance agenda cannot be viewed in isolation with Washington Consensus and second generation reforms. Instead of accepting the failure of neoliberal economic policies, the IFIs shifted the blame on the tardy application of policies in the borrowing countries. By blaming the poor institutions for the failure of the Washington Consensus, the IFIs paved the way for institutional and political reforms through aid conditionalities in the borrowing countries. The borrowing countries are being advised to complement economic reforms (also known as first-generation reforms) with institutional and political reforms — with what are known as second-generation reforms. Since first-generation conditionalities were aimed at liberalizing the economy ('getting prices right'), the second-generation conditionalities refer to redesigning the state and its institutions ('getting institutions right') to ensure smooth development of market economy. Consequently, promotion of good governance has become an integral part of the emergent global economic order.

Democracy Promotion US-style!

The shift towards promotion of democracy at the global level is much more pronounced in the US foreign policy. It is not by mere coincidence that the US has suddenly discovered the virtues of democracy. Since 1945, there have been several American interventions against democratically-elected governments and popular movements. The involvement of the US in the overthrowing of democratically-elected governments — Iran in 1953, Guatemala in 1954, Congo in 1960, Greece in 1967, Chile in 1973 and Fiji in 1987 — is well documented. According to William Blum, the US was involved in the overthrow of more than 40 foreign governments and suppression of over 30 popular movements struggling against authoritarian regimes.[2]

Just as support to client states and right-wing dictatorships and interventions abroad in the post-World War II period marked US foreign policy, promotion of democracy in the third world countries has become the cornerstone of the present era of US foreign policy. The dramatic shift in the US policy was quite visible in Philippines, Zaire and Chile where the US administration supported popular resistance in these countries in the eighties and the nineties. US now spends roughly $700 million every year to promote a particular version of democracy globally through agencies such as the United States Agency for International Development (USAID) and National Endowment for Democracy (NED).

The NED was established in 1983 as a private, nongovernmental donor agency to strengthen democratic institutions in the world. It supports a wide range of civil society institutions including NGOs, trade unions, media, students groups, etc. NED activities with special emphasis on privatization, deregulation and minimalist state intervention are in concurrence with the globalization process. NED has played a crucial role in promoting US version of democracy and free-market economy in Central America, Philippines and Eastern Europe. The role played by NED in manipulating elections in Nicaragua in 1990 and Mongolia in 1996 and dislodging of democratically-elected governments in Bulgaria in 1990 and Albania in 1991 is an open secret.

Notwithstanding its global crusade for democracy promotion, the US government's commitment is governed more by self-interest and short term geo-political exigencies rather than any genuine concern for democracy, as evident from two latest military coups against the democratically elected governments of Nawaz Sharif in Pakistan in 1999 and Hugo Chavez in Venezuela in 2002. In the aftermath of September 11, 2001 attacks, General Musharraf regime became a key ally of the US due to geo-political exigencies and has been consistently praised by the Bush administration in the international fora. Chavez, a left-wing populist and a vocal critic of US foreign policy, was never in the good books of Washington. Chavez's populist measures to distribute land to the landless and imposition of higher taxes on oil companies were resented by big business and a section of well-entrenched middle class and labor aristocracy. Instead of denouncing the coup against Chavez, the

Bush administration justified the coup and even gave tacit support to it by declaring that Chavez "should learn his lessons." However, to US's consternation, Chavez was able to stage a comeback within three days with the support of loyal troops and countrywide popular protests.

Till 1997, the US was supporting the Taliban regime in Afghanistan, known for its heinous violations of human rights and oppression of women. Besides, the US has been extending moral, economic, military and political support to several authoritarian regimes in oil-rich Middle East countries for decades, despite their terrible records on human rights. Al Jazeera, perhaps the only genuinely free television channel in the Arab world, is most detested by the US administration.

Insistence by the US to adopt its version of democracy at the global level also does not mean that the US is an inherently democratic country. The way important economic and political decisions are influenced by powerful corporations and special interest groups in the US (with hardly any input from public) leaves little doubt about the actual practice of democracy within the country. *Businessweek* carried out an interesting survey of corporate power in the US in 2000.[3] The survey revealed several startling facts, some of which are summarized below:

■ 74 per cent said that big business has too much power in influencing government policies, politicians, and policy-makers in Washington.

■ 72 per cent of Americans say business has too much power over too many aspects of American life.

■ 95 per cent were of the opinion that US corporations should have more than one purpose. They said that corporations owe something to their workers and the communities in which they operate and corporations should sacrifice some profit for the benefit of workers and communities.

Not long ago, the US administration strongly criticized the capitalism model pursued by the East Asian countries. It cried hoarse that the East Asian financial crisis is an outcome of 'crony capitalism' (an unholy alliance between corporations and government) and endorsed American model of corporate governance based on 'free enterprise.' Nonetheless, the spate of financial scandals that rocked corporate America in 2002 (e.g., Enron, WorldCom, Xerox, Global Crossing, Tyco International, Adelphia Communications, etc.) has unveiled that crony capitalism is not limited to East Asian countries alone. The US system is as much in the grip of crony capitalism.

The world is by now quite familiar with stories of corporate America doling out millions of dollars in political donations to both Republicans and Democrats. A recent study revealed that business provides $3 out of every $4 raised by Republicans and $2 out of every $3 raised by Democrats as political donations. In return, the US political system reciprocates by granting massive tax cuts and concessions to the very rich. Kevin Phillips, in his seminal work *Wealth and Democracy: A Political History of the American Rich* points to the threats posed by increasing inequality to democracy in the US. He notes, "aftertax incomes for the bottom 60 per cent of Americans declined, with the bottom losing 12 per cent, while aftertax incomes for the top 1 per cent more than doubled between 1997 and 1999." Tax cuts for the wealthiest Americans received a fillip under the Bush administration. The poorest 20 per cent of American taxpayers have received only 1 per cent of the total tax relief amounting to meager $98 to their discretionary income — belying the claims of a 'rising middle class' trumpeted by the Bush administration.

Global Crusade for Democracy or Polyarchy?

The 'third wave' of democratization has not created a clear-cut division between democratic and authoritarian regimes. Rather, it has given rise to a wide range of political regimes which are neither completely democratic nor authoritarian. These regimes are located in the gray zone between genuine democracy and overt authoritarian. Such 'hybrid' regimes have been termed by many political scientists as 'low intensity democracy,' 'illiberal democracy,' 'pseudo democracy,' 'restricted democracy,' 'mechanical democracy' and 'delegative democracy.' Some of the common characteristics of 'hybrid' regimes include unstable government, weak party system, economic insecurity and shallow democratic institutions. Russia, Azerbaijan, Peru, Croatia, Haiti, Paraguay, Mozambique and Ghana are examples of such regimes. These regimes organize periodic elections to gain democratic legitimacy but violate all democratic norms and institutions systematically.

Despite possessing all the formal democratic institutions, democracy as culture is sorely missing in these regimes. Focused exclusively on 'getting elections right' such regimes fail to institutionalize other vital aspects of democratic governance. A US political scientist, Robert A. Dahl, first coined the term 'polyarchy' in the early 1970s to describe such political regimes.[4] Polyarchy refers to a political system in which a small coterie rules while public participation in decision-making is confined to selecting leaders through periodic elections. By confining democratic participation only in terms of voting, polyarchy does not deepen the process of democratization. The components of such a political system include dominance of a coterie of leaders in political parties, popular support based on patronage and absence of inner-party democracy. In other words, polyarchy nullifies the basic principle of democracy — government of the people, by the people and for the people.

Based on 'one person, one vote' principle, it is assumed that this equality is sufficient for democratic order and therefore vital concerns such as economic equality are not given due attention. While developing a strong critique of electoral democracy, one is not belittling the significance of universal suffrage and free and fair elections as an instrument to widen public participation and accountability in decision-making processes. But polyarchy provides no institutional mechanism to hold elected representatives accountable once they come to power. The elected representatives can only be held accountable by being voted out of office in the next elections. Leave alone fulfillment of basic democratic rights and aspirations of people, even important concerns related to elections such as use of money and muscle power, intimidation of electorate, large-scale rigging of ballots, misuse of official machinery, and media manipulations are not given due attention in a polyarchic system.

According to William I. Robinson, polyarchy represents a global political system corresponding to the global economy under the hegemony of transnational elites.[5] The underlying objective of polyarchy is to maintain an unjust and undemocratic society. Rather than facilitating resolution of economic and political conflicts created by elite-based global order, polyarchy acts as a safety valve to deflect popular aspirations generated by mass movements seeking radical democratization of social life. Under a polyarchic regime, there is no threat to *status quo* and the focus is exclusively on democratic form, rather than the democratic content. Such a regime is perceived to be conducive for legitimizing the domination of powerful ruling elites as well as providing political stability desired by transnational capital for its smooth movement across borders.

It is the Quality of Democracy, Stupid!

Notwithstanding globalization of democracy, its quality remains highly questionable. In most nascent democracies, formal democratic institutions have been installed with emphasis on free and periodic elections. The conduct of periodic elections is seen as the sole objective of democratic politics. No doubt, periodic elections are necessary but they are not sufficient to check abuse of power and consolidate democratization. There are several cases, for instance Zimbabwe and Pakistan, where elections and referendums have been tailored to legitimize the continuation of authoritarian regimes. By limiting the concept of democracy to political democracy with emphasis on electoral processes, wider issues such as control over wealth and power, domination by TNCs and finance capital, and inequalities and asymmetries within and among nations are not being addressed as issues of democracy. For the vast majority of people, democracy does not mean only right to vote and curbing of dictatorial tendencies. It also means a better quality of life; an equitable distribution of wealth, income and natural resources; dismantling of highly concentrated structures of property ownership; better employment opportunities; access to housing, health and education; cultural development and so forth.

In this regard, even advanced democracies lack democratic norms. One cannot ignore the fact that poverty and illiteracy rates have remained high in several countries that have been democratic for decades. Regardless of democratic regime in India, social and economic problems of the poor and marginalized sections of society have not been dealt with. The right to vote in India has, so far, not translated into the basic human right to food, work, shelter and livelihood. The occurrence of starvation deaths and widespread

Box 3.2

Foreign Capital and Authoritarian Regimes: Unholy Nexus

Not long ago, foreign capital, both FDI and portfolio, hindered the process of democratic consolidation in many parts of the world. The Cold War era is replete with instances where foreign investors did little to promote democracy and human rights in the host countries. Instead, foreign investors often with the tacit support of their home governments backed the authoritarian regimes and even encouraged dictators to unleash repressive measures to contain political dissent which was perceived as a potential threat to their economic interests. Shell in Nigeria, Unocal in Burma, British Petroleum in Colombia and Freeport McMoran in Indonesia colluded with authoritarian regimes to unleash a reign of terror. While in other instances, TNCs joined hands with the US and other western countries to overthrow those democratically-elected governments which were not friendly to corporate interests. The role of United Fruit in Guatemala and ITT in Chile in orchestrating the toppling of democratically elected governments has been well documented.

International banks played a major role in the transfer of 'dirty money' belonging to dictators and their cronies. Despite being aware of these illegitimate sources of funds, prominent international banks transferred billions of dollars siphoned by Sani Abacha of Nigeria, Mobutu Sese Seko of Zaire and Ferdinand Marcos of Philippines to secret bank accounts in Switzerland and other countries. In addition, billions of dollars lent by the World Bank and the IMF also enabled dictators to loot public money and make their countries poorer than ever.

Authoritarian regimes in Latin America, Africa and Asia received large quantities of foreign direct investment and commercial loans from international banks. By strengthening commercial ties with

contd. on next page

the authoritarian regimes, foreign investors and banks gave a clear message to the world that business takes precedence over any concern for democracy and human rights. On the other hand, dictators used commercial ties with foreign investors and banks to gain legitimacy in the international community. At the domestic level, dictators extended the perks of foreign money to a handful of local elite and loyal army who filled their coffers with the connivance of foreign investors and lenders.

Thus, an unholy nexus took shape through which foreign capital supported authoritarian regimes while such regimes solicited foreign capital to legitimize their repressive measures besides doling out favors to the local elites. South Africa, rich in gold, diamond and mineral resources, was the favorite destination of both FDI and portfolio investments during the apartheid regime in the 1970s and 1980s. Foreign investments in South Africa not only bestowed legitimacy on the apartheid regime but also buttressed the economic domination of the ruling white minority.

chronic malnutrition amidst plenty of food rotting in official warehouses is an indicator of democratic deficit in India, the world's largest democracy.

In the case of countries that have recently incorporated democracy, sharp downtrends in economic growth, income distribution and human development can be witnessed. This phenomenon is vividly evident in Eastern Europe and Central Asia where poverty levels have touched unprecedented heights in the aftermath of formal democratic regimes. The number of people living on less than $1 per day increased from one million in 1987 to 24 million in 1998 in these countries.[6] Russia, in particular, has witnessed upswings in the levels of unequal distribution of income in the recent years — the income share of the richest 20 per cent is 11 times that of the poorest 20 per cent.[7] According to *Forbes* magazine, more billionaires are based in Moscow than any other city in the world.

Increasing concentration in terms of private ownership of property has become the touchstone of almost all democracies. Is it not quixotic that under the dictates of transnational capital, political democracy cohabits with unequal distribution of income and wealth?

No wonder, democracy project is being perceived with skepticism. Disillusionment has replaced the euphoria about democracy that marked the 1980s and early 1990s, as regime change has not led to radical socio-economic transformation. Right to franchise and regular elections offer little solace to the poor masses who expect governments to improve their living conditions. As a consequence, there is an increasing trend towards depoliticization, lower turnouts in elections, and apathy towards social and political issues. In such an environment, the findings of an opinion poll (reported in *The Economist*) that a large number of people in many Latin American countries do not hold democratic political regimes in high esteem are hardly surprising. The highest number of those disenchanted with democracy belonged to Brazil where only 47 per cent of respondents agreed with the statement, "Democracy is preferable to any other form of government." While 18 per cent of respondents said that in some circumstances, authoritarianism was preferable, and 29 per cent thought that it made no difference.

Latino-barometro, a Chilean organization, carried out a similar poll in 2002 which found that Latin Americans have little trust in political parties and believe that corruption has touched its lowest ebb in the past three years. The survey reported that majority of Latin Americans have lost faith in privatization, and want the state to play an active role in regulating the economy. In some countries (e.g., South Korea and Paraguay), recent opinion polls have also reported that the popularity of former dictators remains quite high, as majority of people feel that they were better off under authoritarian regimes than the present democratic ones.

Globalization, Independent Economic Policy-Making and Democratization

There are various reasons to contend that current phase of globalization is not conducive for the promotion and deepening of democracy and human rights. To a large extent, financial liberalization and capital account liberalization — the two important components of globalization — explain the weakening of democratic influence on economic policy-making. The ability of sovereign states to implement independent macroeconomic policies (for instance, monetary policy) has been severely undermined by financial globalization. Mobility of capital across borders has complicated the management of money supply, exchange rates and interest rates at the national level.

Furthermore, fiscal constraints and the 'discipline' imposed by the international financial community influence the scope of pro-poor and redistributive policies. Foreign portfolio investors have the ability to 'vote by foot' by exiting countries that pursue progressive economic policies. Sudden change in the investors' sentiments can trigger volatile movements in interest and exchange rates. A crisis in one country can soon travel to neighboring countries depending on the degree of economic integration. If foreign investors hold a substantial domestic debt, the crisis may soon turn into a fiscal crisis as well. The risks associated with volatile capital flows are well illustrated by financial crises in several emerging markets in the 1990s (Mexico in 1994, East Asia in 1997, Russia and Brazil in 1998, and Turkey in 2000). Here it needs to be emphasized that the domestic counterparts of foreign investors are also not far behind in shunning progressive economic policies.

Financial liberalization and globalization are not the only limiting factors hindering democratic decision-making processes. The fact that several key economic decisions with wider ramifications have been taken by governments to comply with the global trade regime, needs no further elaboration.

There is no denying that economic globalization influences domestic policy options but it would be erroneous to conclude that countries cannot pursue alternative economic policies. To a large extent, it depends on the political will as well as the power of institutions and interest groups within the country. There are countries, for instance China and Malaysia, which have imposed strict controls on capital movements to pursue independent monetary policies. There are several other instances where national governments have undertaken policy measures against the interests of transnational capital.

Delinking of Economic Decision-making from Democratic Political Processes

There are several important factors that influence the scope of democratic decision-making in the economic domain. One such factor is technocratic form of governance through the establishment of arrangements such as independent central banks and regulatory authorities (albeit within the state). Such independent arrangements gives extra-constitutional powers to a handful of technocrats who operate independently of democratic control and accountability. In the neoliberal intellectual climate, economic policy-making is viewed as a highly technical and complicated matter and therefore only technocrats should handle it with no accountability to elected representatives. Undeniably, in the present times, policy-making (in all public matters including health, education and transport) requires greater technical expertise but it should not be at the expense of democratic accountability and control.

Insulation of central banks from democratic control has become the cornerstone of neoliberal orthodoxy. Monetary policy is already beyond democratic control in most developed countries. The US and other developed countries have granted varying degrees of autonomy to their central banks. This means that key economic issues such as interest rates that affect income distribution, employment and growth, have been left to the discretion of independent central banks. The new European Central Bank (ECB) symbolizes this trend. The key economic decisions of all member-countries of the EU are now being handled by the ECB, which is considered as the most powerful central bank in the world. But the ECB is mired by lack of transparency, accountability and democratic control. The minutes of ECB's meetings are not made public. Although decisions taken by the ECB have a profound impact on the lives of ordinary Europeans, they have no clue as to why and how decisions are arrived at the ECB. Is it not hypocritical that developing countries are asked by the international financial institutions to maintain greater transparency and openness while central banks of developed countries continue to operate in secrecy?

In the case of developing world too, technocratic forms of governance are under way in order to delink economic policy-making from democratic political processes. For instance, Brazil, Argentina and Chile have granted greater autonomy to central banks to formulate key economic policies. Several countries including Argentina and Brazil have enacted fiscal responsibility laws to restrain the scope of fiscal policies. In almost all these countries, such fundamental changes have been introduced without much public participation and discussion.

It needs to be emphasized here that the international financial institutions have encouraged the trend towards technocratic control over economic decision-making as a necessary precondition for implementing structural adjustment programs. Particularly, the IMF has been a great votary of the independence of central banks. The Fund suspended the disbursement of scheduled $400 million loan tranche to Indonesia in 2001 when the government proposed amendments in the central bank laws in order to enhance the public accountability of central bank.

Delinking of economic policy-making from the domain of democratic political control is rationalized on the grounds that politicians are more concerned with short-term consequences of their policy choices (for instance, the next election) and therefore they should not be involved in long-term policy-making processes. But this argument is based on the specious assumption that independent central bankers and technocrats are 'neutral' and therefore are not susceptible to pressures.

There is also no evidence to prove that by insulating them from popular control, central banks become independent of financial markets. Experiences show that they are hardly immune to the demands of private financiers who prefer price stability and conservative monetary policies. Like any other class of people, central bankers and technocrats are also not free from lack of competence, biases in favor of special interest groups and corruption. In 1999, for instance, Russian central bank's foreign currency reserves worth $1.7 billion reached a secret firm, Fimaco, based in the British Island of Jersey. In 2001, Syahril Sabirin, the governor of Indonesia's central bank, was jailed for his alleged involvement in siphoning off millions of dollars while in office. Ernst Welteke, President of

Germany's Bundesbank, had to resign in 2004 after the allegation that Dresdner Bank paid his hotel bills in 2001. Similar scandals have been reported in other countries too.

Another argument made by the proponents of independent central banks is that independence leads to better economic performance. In reality, evidence shows that there have been no real improvements in terms of economic growth. An international survey carried out by Alberto Alesina and Lawrence Summers in 1993 found that central bank independence had no measurable impact on real economic performance.

Delinking of economic decision-making from the political processes through technocratic forms of governance is thoroughly undemocratic as it subverts accountability and popular participation in policy-making. By handing over key economic policy-making to unelected and unaccountable central bankers and technocrats, countries weaken democratic influence over economic policy making.[8]

Democratic Deficit from Local to Global Spaces

The growing democratic deficit is deeply manifested in all spheres, local as well as global. There is a growing consensus in the international policy-making circles that a development strategy based on decentralization and local self-governance (granting more powers to local bodies and governments) is the key to prosperity. Several critics of globalization also believe that decentralization coupled with localization of economy can not only resist the globalization process but also has the potential to usher in genuine democratization. Some even view civil society as an alternative to state and consider the retreat of state from the public affairs as a positive development for the deepening of democracy and promotion of human rights. Such naïve thinking is oblivious to the fact that civil society includes an assortment of collective groups — from religious entities to business associations. Not all such civil society organizations are run on democratic principles or pay heed to minimum standards of transparency and accountability.

The new development paradigm presents democratic local governance as a substitute to state intervention in alleviating poverty and ensuring economic growth. The international donor community has shown special interest in supporting local governance projects throughout the world. In the 1990s, the US official aid agency, USAID, supported 60 'local governance' initiatives while UNDP supported more than 250 decentralization projects. In contrast, experiences show that decentralization agenda has little to do with genuine democratization of economic decision-making processes since crucial matters are decided by a handful of technocrats and political elites without any semblance of public debate and discussion. In the name of decentralization and local self-governance, essential developmental tasks and social responsibilities of the state are being handed over to cash-starved, non-transparent, unaccountable NGOs and local bodies without examining their performance and capacity to deliver. While neoliberal globalization is influencing the nation-state from above, the welfare functions of nation-state are also being weakened from below in the guise of decentralization, mushrooming of welfare-oriented NGOs, charities, self-help groups, microfinance programs, etc. There are ample examples of this trend throughout Latin America, Africa and Asia.

Evidence reveals that there is nothing inherently democratic about local bodies and NGOs. Stories related to misappropriation of funds, incompetence, and biases in favor of certain interest groups by local bodies and NGOs are not uncommon. Further, one cannot overlook the fact that transnational capital has the capability of building 'partnerships' with the local ruling elite who could be as inaccessible and unaccountable to the public as their national and international counterparts. There are several instances where TNCs, while working in partnership with NGOs, have actually thwarted peoples' empowerment and developmental initiatives. Besides, corporate donations to philanthropic NGOs has more to do with value addition to brands and enhancement of public image of TNCs. NGOs are being used, inadvertently or otherwise, by TNCs to penetrate the rural markets through self-help groups and microfinance institutions. TNCs involved in consumer goods, agricultural and pharmaceutical businesses view such institutions as a tool to make inroads into the rural markets.

In contrast to local spaces, democratic deficit is even more apparent at the global spaces. The present global policy arrangements in the fields of finance, production, trade, communication, environment are bereft of genuine democratization. There are a host of inter-state arrangements operating at global level without any semblance of popular participation, consultation, transparency and accountability. The list includes BIS, EU, NATO, IMF, World Bank, ADB, APEC, IADB, MERCOSUR, OECD, WTO, G-7, G-20, to mention a few. In most cases, powerful states exert considerable influence over these arrangements. Take the case of G-7. This grouping plays a dominating role in the management of world economy by influencing interest rates, exchange rates and policies related to the IMF and World Bank. But the membership of the grouping is restricted to a handful of powerful states whose total population is not even 11 per cent of the world population. Like the G-7, the BIS and the OECD also have an overbearing influence in steering global financial flows and economic decision-making processes though they overwhelmingly represent the creditor countries. Both these institutions have very weak democratic credentials and formal mechanisms of public participation.

Despite having more than 180 member-countries, the IMF and the World Bank follow an undemocratic structure of governance. Voting rights in the World Bank and IMF are still governed by the archaic rules framed in 1944. In the World Bank, votes are weighted according to the amount of money each country subscribes to it. Each member-country has 250 votes plus one additional vote for every share that it holds, each worth $100000. Members buy shares by subscribing money to the Bank. Any amendment in Bank's rules requires 85 per cent of the votes. The US being the largest shareholder with over 17 per cent votes can veto any amendment. While China and India together have only 5 per cent of the total votes, although they represent 36 per cent of the world's population. In the case of IMF, a similar undemocratic structure ensures that the developed countries have an effective say in decision-making. These institutions still follow an archaic practice under which the President of the World Bank is the nominee of the US while an European nominee heads the IMF.

Under their Articles of Agreement, the World Bank and the IMF are not supposed to enter into policy conditionality and restructuring of the economy of the member-countries. But both institutions have expanded their policy conditionality since the 1980s. Not only the number of conditionalities has increased but also their scope has widened beyond core monetary and fiscal macroeconomic issues. Now with the incorporation of governance and institutional reforms, the mandate of the IFIs have been further widened.

In spite of large-scale expansion in their operations, IFIs are yet to make any headway on the accountability front. Under strong pressure generated by civil society, the IFIs have undertaken measly reforms in the last few years in terms of transparency and consultation. Yet these reforms are not adequate for ensuring wider accountability, both vertical (staff to Exec tive Board) and horizontal. Both these institutions remain secretive and unaccountable.

In the case of a presumably democratically constituted United Nations, the principle of 'one country, one vote' is applicable in the General Assembly but the power of veto granted to the five permanent members of the Security Council is without any democratic rationale. In fact, the track record of the UN in resolving international conflicts has been far below expectations as certain powerful member-states have overtly undermined the authority and neutrality of this body.

Compared with the Bretton Woods institutions and the UN, the structure of WTO (with 148 members) may appear to be more democratic as it is based on 'one country, one vote' principle. Besides, all decisions are taken by consensus. In practice, however, the developed countries have disproportionate influence over the WTO and they have been largely dictating its agenda. The dispute settlement mechanism of the WTO is beyond the reach of financial and human resource capabilities of several developing and poor countries given the fact that over 20 member-countries have no permanent representation in Geneva, the headquarters of WTO.

One of the notable features of democratic deficit in global space is the sheer neglect of public participation in the formulation of policies of international institutional arrangements. Forget about the authoritarian regimes, even those countries who claim to be democratic have failed to inform their own citizens about their involvement with several global institutions.

In addition, there are a host of private agencies active in global governance arena such as International Accounting Standards Committee and Moody's Investors Service. Such private agencies have

Box 3.3

Globalized Media: Shrinking of Public Space?

It is well recognized that communication and media play a significant role in advancing democracy. Facilitated by new technological innovations, the global media industry is undergoing rapid transformation with the growing trend towards concentration and formation of conglomerates controlled by a handful of TNCs.[10] Electronic media, in particular television, has become the most powerful medium of communication. It is estimated that there are over 1.5 billion TV sets around the world with hundreds of satellite channels providing entertainment 24-hours a day. In an advertisement-based, profit-driven commercial media, public space for information exchange and discussions, so essential to a democratic society, is getting further constricted. Throughout the world, there has been a weakening of public broadcasting systems, with negative consequences for the public space. Robert W. McChesney in his highly acclaimed book, *Rich Media, Poor Democracy*, has delineated the impact of corporate media on democracy in the US.[11] According to him, the more powerful and wealthy corporate media giants, the poorer are the prospects for participatory democracy. This trend is also discernible in many parts of the world.

While critically commenting on the role of global media, one cannot deny that new opportunities to promote democracy and human rights may open up by certain processes. For instance, the use of emails and Internet has helped several pro-democracy activists and groups to share information and launch international campaigns against violation of human rights. Not long ago, anti-corporate activists used Internet as a medium to launch a campaign against Multilateral Agreement of Investment (MAI). Under the influence of this campaign, to a large extent, the OECD had to shelve this proposed treaty. With the increased networking of grassroot activists and groups through email and Internet, the operations of TNCs have come under close scrutiny. Despite regulatory and access concerns, the potential of Internet as part of a wider struggle for democratization of media needs to be debated.

no formal mechanisms of public accountability.

Given the failure of existing international institutions, some analysts have proposed new institutions to resolve contemporary conflicts. Some of the notable proposed institutions are Global Parliament, World Financial Authority and Global Tax Organization.[9] The proposals for the creation of new international institutional arrangements certainly merit attention because of the limited mandate of the existing ones. But the problems plaguing the existing institutional arrangements cannot be addressed by the mere creation of new entities. For instance, a Global Parliament is not a substitute to national parliamentary system. Asking billions of citizens to elect a global parliament through multiparty elections in all parts of the world is preposterous, as citizens have absolutely no clue how the complex operations of global structures affect their daily lives.

Given the unequal international power relations, the new global institutional arrangements could be as secret, undemocratic and unaccountable as the existing ones. A just global order cannot be constructed by creating new institutional arrangements alone. Therefore, the real challenge lies in fundamentally restructuring and democratizing the international power relations that govern existing international institutional arrangements.

Globalization and Onslaught on Democratic Rights

One of the most damaging consequences of economic globalization has been a systematic onslaught on workers' rights. There is hardly any region or country where democratic rights of the workers have not come under severe attack by the processes of globalization. Even die-hard advocates of globalization admit that adjustment policies cause large-scale unemployment, greater income inequalities and economic hardship.

In several countries, investor-friendly labor laws curtailing the basic rights of the workers to organize and form labor unions have been introduced to attract transnational capital. In countries like India and South Korea where labor unions have some political clout, there has been resistance to such proposals. Whereas in certain other countries (e.g., Thailand, Pakistan, Nigeria and Chile), investment-friendly labor laws have already been promulgated without much resistance. In many developing countries, labor unions have been legally banned from export processing zones. The pathetic working conditions of workers (particularly women workers) in export-processing zones require hardly any elaboration. The plight of workers in the informal sector is as abysmal.

Adjustment policies involve several policy measures which adversely affect the working classes. Due to privatization, closures, mergers and acquisitions and swift changes in the production processes (such as sub-contracting and informalization of economy), workers' bargaining power is getting further weakened which, in turn, weakens their political power. Besides, orthodox tight monetary and fiscal policies have also contributed towards diluting the bargaining power of workers. This has important consequences for democratic polity because the working class played a dominant role, often in alliance with other social and political movements, in the establishment of democracy and welfare state in several countries. In several countries such as South Africa and South Korea, democracy was attained largely due to the protracted struggles launched by labor unions. By weakening the rights of pro-democracy groups such as organized labor unions, economic globalization dampens the continuing process of democratization.

In many countries, economic policies with far reaching impact on the lives of citizens have been implemented without public consultation and debate. Not only authoritarian regimes but even democratic regimes have fallen short of seeking public approval on important economic policy matters. In India, for instance, significant economic policy decisions have been taken bypassing the state legislative assemblies and the Parliament. India signed the IMF adjustment program in 1991 and joined the WTO in 1994 without even seeking approval from the Parliament, let alone public participation and wider consultation.

Concluding Remarks

To sum up, genuine democracy cannot be ushered in without a radical restructuring of the contemporary globalization processes. Democratic values like human dignity, freedom, equity and justice cannot take root in a polity obsessed with neoliberal orthodoxy.

The world, in fact, needs a much more open discourse on globalization and democracy, than what has been offered by mass media, academia and research institutions. The contours of public discourse can be enlarged by a variety of policy measures such as promotion of independent public broadcasting systems, democratization of universities and cultural institutions, curbs on the monopoly ownership of media, expanding the space for informed political discussion through local media and so forth. These measures would go a long way in strengthening public participation on issues concerning contemporary social life. For that to happen, the role of a democratic and accountable state is predominant in deepening the democratization process at all levels.

Notes and References

1. UNRISD, *Visible Hands: Taking Responsibility for Social Development*, Geneva, 2000, p. 42.

2. William Blum, *Rogue State: A Guide to the World's Only Superpower*, Zed Books, London, 2003, p. 2.

3. Aaron Bernstein, "Too Much Corporate Power," *Businessweek*, September 11, 2000.

4. Robert A. Dahl, *Polyarchy: Participation and Opposition*, Yale University Press, New Haven, 1971.

5. The linkages of polyarchy and neoliberal globalization have been delineated in William I. Robinson, *Promoting Polyarchy: Globalization, US Intervention, and Hegemony*, Cambridge University Press, Cambridge, 1996.

6. UNRISD, op.cit., p. 50.

7. UNDP, *Human Development Report 1999*, Oxford University Press, New York, 1999, p. 31.

8. For a critique of central bank independence and its adverse impact on democracy, see Sheri Berman and Kathleen R. McNamara, "Bank on Democracy: Why Central Banks need Public Oversight," *Foreign Affairs*, March/April 1999, pp. 2-8.

9. For detailed arguments in favor of establishing a global parliament, see Richard Falk and Andrew Strauss, "Toward Global Parliament," *Foreign Affairs*, January/February, 2001, pp. 212-220. The idea of a World Finance Authority has been proposed by John Eatwell and Lance Taylor in their book, *Global Finance at Risk: The Case for International Regulation*, Polity Press, Cambridge, 2000. Vito Tanzi, former head of fiscal affairs department at the IMF, has been a strong supporter for setting up a World Tax Organization. For a detailed account of his proposal, see Vito Tanzi, *Taxation in an Integrating World*, Brookings Institution, Washington, 1995; and Vito Tanzi, "Does the World Need a World Tax Organization?," in Assaf Razin and Efraim Sadka (eds.), *The Economics of Globalization*, Cambridge University Press, Cambridge, 1999, pp. 173-186.

10. For a detailed account on media monopoly by a handful of transnational corporations and the struggle for democratic communications, see Edward S. Herman and Robert W. McChesney, *The Global Media: The New Missionaries of Corporate Capitalism*, Madhyam Books, Delhi, 1997.

11. Robert W. McChesney, *Rich Media, Poor Democracy: Communication Politics in Dubious Times*, University of Illinois Press, Urbana and Chicago, 1999.

CHAPTER 4

International Aid, IFIs and Good Governance: Whose Governance Matters?

> Good governance means enforcing laws and contracts fairly, respecting human rights and property rights, and fighting corruption. Encouraging economic freedom means removing barriers to trade with neighbors and the world, opening the economy to foreign and domestic investment and competition, and divesting government from business operations. Economic freedom also means recognizing that it is the private sector that creates prosperity, not central planning or bureaucracies.
>
> *Paul O'Neill*
> former Treasury Secretary of the US.[1]

OF late, the terms 'governance' and 'good governance' have become buzzwords in the development discourse. Strong arguments have been proffered from various quarters that without 'good governance' structures, the poor and the developing countries cannot achieve economic growth or reduce poverty. Bad governance is being increasingly viewed as the main cause behind all ills confronting these societies. By linking governance as a conditionality for development aid, the international donor community has foregrounded governance issues.

Pushed by the powerful international financial institutions, 'good governance' has become the cornerstone of development cooperation. The World Bank, in particular, has been a leading votary of 'good governance.'[2] Nowadays it is difficult to come across aid packages of multilateral financial institutions and bilateral donors that do not use the term 'good governance' and contain 'governance' conditionalities. There have been several instances in the past few years where aid packages have been suspended on account of 'poor governance.' Sierra Leone, Cameroon, Haiti, Fiji, Liberia and Zimbabwe are the latest examples. Several transnational corporations (TNCs) have pulled out from countries (for instance, Burma and Russia) which they perceived as 'poorly governed.' Calpers, the largest US pension fund with over $160 billion in assets, ruled out investing in several emerging markets (for instance, Indonesia, Malaysia, China, Colombia and Russia) because of poor governance norms and standards.

To examine the shift in the policies of international aid community towards 'good governance' both as an objective and a precondition for development aid, let us begin by defining the concept of 'governance.'

Defining 'Governance' and 'Good Governance'

Notwithstanding popular usage of terms 'governance' and 'good governance,' these are not amenable to precise definitions. The development aid community is yet to define the contours of 'governance' and 'good governance.' 'Governance' may imply different meanings to different people. From NGOs and community organizations to powerful states and multilateral institutions — all swear by good governance. The grounds for supporting 'governance' are as diverse as their avowed proponents. Consequently, one finds that a variety of definitions, often at cross-purposes, are being used to describe 'governance,' thereby further confounding the concept.

Technically speaking, the term 'governance' has been derived from the Greek word, *kybernan*, meaning 'to steer and to pilot or be at the helm of things.' *American Heritage Dictionary* (2000) defines governance as "the act, process, or power of governing." Put simply, 'governance' means processes through which decisions are made and implemented. The concept of 'good governance' conveys the qualitative dimension of governance. Attempts to define what constitutes good or bad governance have failed in the past because concepts and processes of 'governance' vary from country to country. For instance, a corrupt practice in one country such as insider trading, tax evasion and money laundering may be considered as normal business practice in another. Due to lack of precise definition, the debate over the use of term 'governance' instead of government remains inconclusive.[3]

In World Bank's definition, 'governance' encompasses the form of political regime; the process by which authority is exercised in the management of a country's economic and social resources for development; and the capacity of governments to design, formulate and implement policies and discharge functions. The Bank has defined 'good governance' with six main characteristics:

1. Voice and accountability, which includes civil liberties and political stability;
2. Government effectiveness, which includes the quality of policy making and public service delivery;
3. The quality of regulatory framework;
4. The rule of law, which includes protection of property rights;
5. Independence of the judiciary; and
6. Curbing corruption.[4]

As evident from the above-mentioned characterization, the Bank tends to equate 'governance' within the ambit of government with an emphasis on corruption, transparency, participation and rule of law. Thus, the Bank's governance-related programs are concerned with public sector management, public administration, downsizing of bureaucracy and the privatization of state-owned companies. Without belittling the importance of these measures, the fact remains that such a narrow approach cannot help in understanding the myriad issues related to the concept of 'good governance.' The Bank as well as international donor community is oblivious to the relationship between 'good governance' and attainment of basic economic, social and political rights. With an emphasis on technocratic approaches, important issues related to politics and power relations both within and among countries are not given due attention. In fact, it is due to World Bank's financial clout and intellectual hegemony, its definition of 'good governance' has gained wider currency within the dominant academic, diplomatic and development cooperation circles.

The Soaring Graph of 'Good Governance' Agenda

The World Bank first used this concept in its 1989 report, *Sub-Saharan Africa: From Crisis to Sustainable Growth*, in which it characterized the crisis confronting the region as a "crisis of governance" and linked ineffectiveness of aid with governance issues. Since then, Africa has become the epicenter of debates on governance. In the following years, the Bank enlarged its policy arena by including good governance as a core element of its development strategy.

However, the major ideological push towards using good governance as a conditionality was formulated by the World Bank in its 1998 report, *Assessing Aid: What Works, What Doesn't, and Why*. In this report, the Bank explained the interaction between development aid and the quality of governance. The report forcefully argued that the impact of aid on growth depends on "sound economic management" and effective institutions. The report endorsed a selective approach to the disbursement of aid based on policy performance and reform commitment, rather than on the extent of poverty or developmental needs of a borrowing country. The report also called upon the Bank to give more financial resources and expertise on governance issues for achieving development goals in the borrowing countries.

In consonance with the new thinking, the Bank has carried out amendments in its operational guidelines to give more importance to good governance in its lending programs. Since 1999, the Bank has also been carrying out Institutional and Governance Reviews (IGR) to assess the quality of governance. The Bank has developed governance indicators to measure governance in more than 150 member-countries.[5] Apart from the fact that the quality of governance cannot be measured in quantitative terms, the problem with governance indicators is that they are mostly geared towards foreign investors and lenders for assessing political risks in countries where they invest. Rather than addressing these issues to people at large for whom governance really matters. Further, these indicators have yet to demonstrate a linear relationship between the quality of governance and development goals. For instance, how can better rule of law contribute towards lowering illiteracy and infant mortality rates?

The World Bank and the IMF are relying on traditional approaches of punitive conditionalities to promote governance and institutional reforms. The growing interest of IFIs on the question of good governance is amply reflected in several Poverty Reduction Strategy Papers (PRSPs)[6] (see Box 4.1). Besides the IFIs, a number of other agencies such as UNDP have jumped onto the bandwagon of good governance. Several major bilateral donor agencies are

Box 4.1   **PRSPs and Good Governance**

Benin: "Improve governance... national anti-corruption strategy... reforming the civil service and ... quickening the pace of decentralization."

Bolivia: "Modernize the State and fight corruption... reform of the judicial system... promote the participation of the private sector in areas previously assumed by the public sector... reduce red tape and bureaucracy in public entities,... decentralization ... transfer political power to municipal governments."

Burkina Faso: "Redefinition of the role of the State... promote good governance... accelerate reforms to strengthen democratic forums and promote the efficient management and transparency of government finance... local governance... combat corruption... reform of the judicial system... decentralization... comprehensive reform of the civil service... better management of public finances."

Ethiopia: "Decentralization and empowerment, judiciary and civil service reform, and institutional capacity building. Judicial and civil service reform will have the effect of encouraging private sector in particular, while decentralization and empowerment will mainly encourage the smallholder farmer."

Guyana: "Good governance and an improved business environment are essential for accountability, transparency and the restoration of business confidence... In the public sector, the goal will be the efficient delivery of services to the private sector by all government ministries and agencies... Government will eliminate redundant positions and reduce vacant positions in the establishment from over 25000 to 12000.... Improving the rule of law."

Kenya: "Good governance is a fundamental building block of a just and economically prosperous society and therefore, is an essential component of action to reduce poverty.... A sustained drive against corruption... reforming the public service... reduced workforce...

contd. on next page

restructuring and retrenchment... Completion of the civil service retrenchment exercise to reduce the service by at least 48000."

Mali: "Creating an enabling regulatory, legislative, and institutional framework... strengthening democracy and the rule of law; implementing the decentralization policy... public sector restructuring and privatization... good governance... fight to end corruption."

Malawi: "Civil service reform... retrenchment of 20000 temporary employees... improve financial management and accountability... good governance... decentralization process... democratic environment... rationalizing government ministries, departments, and agencies... improve financial management and accountability."

increasingly following the performance-based system under which the allocation of aid is linked to the government's performance in terms of reducing poverty. At the UN Conference on Financing for Development at Monterrey (Mexico), the US President, George W. Bush pledged an additional five billion dollars in aid beginning in 2004 to countries which undertake political, legal and economic reforms.[7] Under the New Partnership for Africa's Development (NEPAD) initiative, the linkages between poverty reduction and good governance have been made explicit.[8] The international initiatives aimed at reducing debt burden of the poorest countries [including the Köln Debt Initiative and the Highly Indebted Poor Countries (HIPC) initiative] also link debt relief with governance reforms.

In addition, the agenda of good governance and structural conditionality has played a prominent role in the G-7 Summits. The G-7 leaders have encouraged the IFIs to take an active role in governance reform and institutional development in the borrowing countries through lending, investment and technical assistance activities. By concentrating solely on the quantitative aspects of conditionality and performance indicators, G-7 leaders have not paid adequate attention to the content of conditionalities and the manner in which these are imposed on the borrowing countries. It appears that the G-7 leaders have abandoned long-standing issues such as the reform of the international financial architecture and internal governance of the IFIs which were brought into center stage in the aftermath of the Southeast Asian financial crisis in 1997. The shift in the policies of international aid community, particularly of the IFIs, towards good governance both as an objective and a precondition for development aid is a disturbing phenomenon and needs to be rigorously questioned.

From Washington Consensus to Post-Washington Consensus

Any analysis of good governance would remain incomplete without acknowledging the prominent role of Washington Consensus.[9] It is no coincidence that the concept of good governance gained currency when market-oriented structural adjustment programs pushed by the IFIs in the poor and the developing world were increasingly coming under public scrutiny and criticism. In fact, good governance agenda is deeply embedded in the Washington Consensus.

The benefits assured by Washington Consensus are yet to be realized in spite of its implementation in over a hundred countries since the 1980s. While the negative consequences of this global policy regime at the macroeconomic level as well as on the lives of poor people have been well documented and therefore need no elaboration here. Based on neoclassical economic model, adjustment policies failed miserably to achieve stated objectives of higher economic growth and reduction in poverty. Rather, these policies contributed in no small measure towards worsening of income inequalities in the countries which vigorously implemented it. Instead of accepting the failure of neoliberal economic policies, the IFIs shifted the blame on the tardy application of policies in the borrowing countries. By blaming the poor institutions for the failure of the Washington Consensus, the IFIs paved the way for institutional and political reforms through aid conditionalities in the borrowing countries.

The borrowing countries are being advised to complement economic reforms (also known as first-generation reforms) with institutional and political reforms, which are also known as second-generation reforms.[10] Since first-generation conditionalities were aimed at liberalizing the economy ('getting prices right'), the second-generation conditionalities refer to redesigning the state and its institutions ('getting institutions right') to ensure smooth development of market economy. The second-generation conditionalities have been labeled as structural conditionality in the case of the IMF and governance conditionality in the case of the World Bank.

It is important to emphasize here that the governance agenda reinforces the Washington Consensus through institutional and political conditionalities. Since markets do not function in a vacuum, a rule-based legal regime is necessary for the smooth functioning of market economy. Legal and institutional reforms are oriented towards securing private property rights, enforcing contracts and expansion of private sector. In the present context of globalization, diverse forms of legal, administrative and political systems are considered as impediments in the smooth functioning of a global market economy. That is why, IFIs and the WTO are insisting on harmonized national political, institutional and legal processes in order to ensure smooth operations of transnational capital. The new emphasis on 'sound economic management' may appear a laudable goal but is nothing more than a rigid adherence to fiscal austerity measures. Even the limited concerns for safety nets are attempts to contain mass uprisings against the neoliberal economic order rather than making people economically independent and empowered. No wonder, promotion of good governance has become an integral part of the emergent global economic order.

A recent report by the UNCTAD titled, *From Adjustment to Poverty Reduction: What is New?*, critically examines the new agenda in the context of poverty reduction in Africa.[11] Based on an appraisal of 27 PRSPs in Africa, the report concluded that the macroeconomic policy content of the PRSPs shows "no fundamental departure from the kind of policy advice espoused under what has come to be known as the 'Washington Consensus.'" Efforts aimed at reexamining the governance issues should fundamentally question the orthodoxy of the Washington Consensus that has dominated economic development paradigm since the 1980s.

IFIs and Governance Conditionalities

Conditional aid is not a new phenomenon but when it is used by the external aid agencies to fundamentally alter the institutions and processes of governance in the borrowing countries, it raises several pertinent questions. As in the case of economic reforms, the IFIs are using aid conditionalities to promote good governance in the borrowing countries. With the enlargement of the governance agenda in the eighties and the nineties, the scope of governance conditionalities has also expanded. Since 1996, the Bank has launched over 600 governance related programs and initiatives in 95 countries and is currently involved in several governance and public sector reforms in over 50 countries.[12] The range of Bank's programs with governance related conditionalities include public sector reforms, transparency, civil service reforms, decentralization of delivery system, and legal and judicial reforms.

In the case of the IMF, the share of programs with structural conditions and the average number of conditions per program have increased significantly during 1989-99. According to the IMF's 2001 report titled, *Structural Conditionality in Fund-Supported Programs*, the share of programs with structural conditions has increased from 60 to 100 per cent and the average number of structural conditions per program has increased from 3 to 12. On behalf of G-24, Devesh Kapur and Richard Webb have carried out a comprehensive study of governance related conditionalities of the IFIs.[13] They pointed out that governance related conditionalities represent the bulk of the conditions imposed by the IFIs during 1997-99 – on an average 72 per cent in Africa, 58 per cent in Asia, 59 per cent in Central Asia and Eastern Europe, and 53 per cent in Latin America and the Caribbean (see Tables 4.1 and 4.2). In addition, the report noted that under a narrow definition of conditionality, the burden is most acute in Central Asia and East Europe, whereas a broader definition of conditionality places the greatest burden on sub-Saharan Africa.[14]

According to Kapur and Webb, "Even if conditionality is interpreted narrowly, its burden on borrowers has grown significantly. The average number of criteria for a sample of 25 countries having a program with the IMF in 1999, with programs initiated between 1997 and 1999, is 26. This compares to about six in the 1970s and ten in the 1980s."[15] To illustrate the domination of governance conditionalities, the authors cited the case of IMF's 1997 program with Indonesia that contained 81 conditions, of which 48 pertained to governance. While a similar IMF program in 1999 with Kyrgyzstan contained 97 governance related conditions out of a total 130 conditions. Interestingly, most of the conditionalities were related to the fiscal sector.

Table 4.1: The Burden of Conditionality

	Conditionality Strictly Defined			Conditionality Loosely Defined		
	Total conditionalities (average)	Of which governance related conditionalities	As a percentage of total conditionalities	Total conditionalities (average)	Of which governance related conditionalities	As a percentage of total conditionalities
Africa	23	9	39	114	82	72
Asia	17	4	24	84	49	58
Central Asia and East Europe	36	4	67	93	55	59
Latin America	33	13	39	78	41	53

Source: Devesh Kapur and Richard Webb, *Governance-Related Conditionalities of the International Financial Institutions*, UNCTAD, G-24 Discussion Paper Series 6, UNCTAD, New York and Geneva, 2000. Data based on IMF *Letters of Intent* and *Policy Framework Papers* (PFPs) between 1997 and 1999 for a sample of 25 countries that had a program with the IMF in 1999: Africa: Cameroon, Djibouti, Gambia, Ghana, Guinea, Madagascar, Mali, Mozambique, Rwanda, Senegal, Uganda, Tanzania, Zambia; Asia: Cambodia, Indonesia, Republic of Korea, Thailand; Central Asia and East Europe: Kazakhstan, Kyrgyzstan, Latvia, Romania; Latin America: Bolivia, Brazil, Nicaragua.

The Problem with Governance Conditionalities

The shift towards promoting good governance both as an objective and a precondition for development aid in the borrowing countries is misconceived. Firstly, the shift indicates a radical departure of the IFIs from their traditional responsibilities as mentioned in their Articles of Agreement.[16] Secondly, it is debatable as to whose governance should actually be questioned. Unfortunately, the dominant debate within the international aid community has been on the quantum of aid and conditionality, without fundamentally questioning the *raison d'être* of aid conditionality. The recent experience is a grim reminder that aid conditionality cannot be an appropriate tool for achieving the intended objectives. In a series of articles on this issue, Carlos Santiso has questioned the effectiveness of conditional aid in altering the institutions of governance in the borrowing countries.[17]

Experience with aid conditionality in the context of adjustment lending has also confirmed that conditional aid had very limited influence in their successful implementation. A study by Paul Mosley, Jane Harrigan and John Toye on the World Bank's policy lending has demonstrated that there is no discernible relation between the intensity of conditionality and success in implementation of promised reforms.[18] This finding has been substantiated by the World Bank's own case-studies on aid and reforms in African countries which state that aid cannot buy reform and that the conditionality attached to adjustment loans failed to induce policy changes.[19]

On the other hand, there are several instances where externally enforced economic and political reforms through the instrumentality of conditional aid have seriously undermined the domestic democratic processes in the borrowing countries. Based on a study

Table 4.2: Examples of the Burden of Governance Conditionality

Region	Countries	Conditionality Strictly Defined			Conditionality Loosely Defined		
		Total	Governance related conditionalities	In percentage	Total	Governance related conditionalities	In percentage
Africa	Mali	26	13	50	105	67	64
	Mozambique	22	12	55	74	58	78
	Senegal	27	9	33	165	99	60
	Zambia	18	6	33	87	59	68
Asia	Cambodia	30	9	30	83	65	78
	Indonesia	18	8	44	81	48	59
	Rep. Of Korea	10	4	40	114	44	39
	Kazakhstan	27	17	63	114	69	61
Eastern Europe	Albania	43	33	77	72	47	65
	Latvia	28	20	71	65	28	43
	Romania	43	25	58	82	34	41
Latin America	Brazil	38	21	55	89	45	51
	Bolivia	32	21	66	95	44	46
	Nicaragua	29	18	62	50	34	68

Source: Same as in Table 4.1.

of adjustment lending in South East Asia and Latin America, Tony Killick has debunked the notion that conditionality can "buy" better policies and promote sound governance institutions.[20] The Bank's own researchers have also reported that aid dependence can significantly undermine the quality of governance in the borrowing countries. In an empirical study on aid dependence and quality of governance, Stephen Knack of the World Bank found that aid has led to increased corruption, draining of scarce talent from the bureaucracy, and weakening of institutional capacity and accountability.[21]

Thirdly, it is difficult to measure countries in terms of either good or bad governance. In reality, most of the poor and the developing countries stand somewhere in between. Moreover, there is no guarantee that good governance institutions would automatically lead to reduction of poverty and promotion of sustainable development. We cannot overlook the fact that poverty, infant mortality and illiteracy rates have remained high in several countries that have established democratic governance norms and institutions for decades. For instance, India has not been able to reduce poverty despite having strong democratic governance institutions and processes such as free press, civil liberties, independent judiciary and rule of law. On the other hand, one finds that rapid economic growth and massive reduction in poverty levels occurred in several Asian countries (for instance, China and Malaysia) under poor governance structures and authoritarian regimes.

Despite the growing evidence (emanating from diverse sources including the Bank researchers) against the effectiveness of conditional aid, the IFIs are yet to revisit their intellectual moorings and acknowledge that aid conditionality is not a credible mechanism to usher in policy reforms in the borrowing countries.

The Limits of Technocratic Approach

The governance reforms agenda of the international aid community, particularly of the IFIs, is problematic. Focused exclusively on improving domestic institutions, the technocratic approach does not take into account important external factors (such as protectionism, declining commodity prices, external debt, and volatile capital flows) that act as major impediments in poverty reduction in the poor and the developing world. Thus, it is highly debatable as to whose governance should actually be questioned.

The technocratic approach is based on the premise that liberalization, deregulation and globalization policies hold the key to economic growth which, in turn, would lead to poverty reduction. The emphasis is on liberalization and deregulation of domestic financial markets encompassing market-determined exchange and interest rates; liberalization of current and capital accounts; and granting more autonomy to central bankers and financial regulators. One of the justifications given in favor of market-led reforms is that it would ultimately benefit the poor people. Although the IFIs have yet to demonstrate how financial liberalization helps the poor to come out of the clutches of poverty. To illustrate, while advocating financial liberalization, microfinance is touted as a panacea for poverty reduction by the development aid community. As discussed in Chapter 1, the success of microfinance in reducing poverty is extremely limited and is usually dependent on other developmental efforts which are undermined by the adjustment policies.

Freeing of financial regulators from democratic accountability and control, in fact, exemplifies the growing trend towards technocratic forms of governance goaded by the IFIs. In particular, the IMF has been vociferously encouraging technocratic control over economic decision-making (such as independent central banks) as a necessary precondition for implementing structural adjustment policies. In several countries, central banks and financial regulators have been granted greater autonomy to formulate key economic policies while in some countries (for instance, Argentina and Brazil) fiscal responsibility laws have been enacted to restrain the scope of fiscal policies. This means that key economic issues such as interest rates, exchange rates and monetary policies have been left to the discretion of technocrats. Delinking of economic decision-making from the political processes through such technocratic forms of governance is thoroughly undemocratic as it subverts democratic accountability and popular participation in policy-making.

Implantation of Anglo-American institutions of governance is the overarching theme of the new agenda. It is based on the assumption that the developed countries have the best institutions which could be implanted across the world irrespective of cultural and historical conditions. Implantation of uniform blueprints without addressing underlying power relations and cultural differences is not only ineffective but proves counterproductive. Russia's experience with democracy is a classic example. Democracy can not (and should not) be implanted or imposed through stringent conditionalities by external donors, it has to be imbibed and nurtured from within. That is why, there is no universal model of democracy. The democratic processes vary from country to country because societies differ in terms of history, culture and popular aspirations.

Recent experiences of democracy promotion in several nascent democracies reveal that democratization cannot be achieved through technical approaches aimed at replicating the western models or through technical kits such as training of parliamentarians, civil servants and judges. The top-down technical approach overlooks the fact that democratization is essentially a political issue, which could only be addressed by domestic popular mobilization. Without taking into account the underlying power relations and socio-economic matrix, technical approaches by themselves are hardly adequate for the realization of democracy. It must also be noted that democratization is not a smooth process as it could generate new conflicts based on class, caste, gender and identity.

One of the key components of technocratic approaches towards good governance is policy 'ownership.' In principle, one cannot disagree with the new emphasis on policy 'ownership' but if the latest experience with PRSPs is any indicator, ownership is largely oriented towards ensuring that the borrowing countries do not lag behind in terms of implementation. The report by UNCTAD on poverty reduction in the context of Africa stated that ownership is restricted to the design of safety nets without touching the macroeconomic policies and development strategies.[22] After detecting the strong influence of the IMF and the World Bank on macroeconomic issues in several PRSPs, the report questioned whether policies are truly 'owned' or merely designed to serve the requirements of donors.

The donor community cannot remain oblivious to the fact that conditionality tends to undermine countries' ownership of reforms rather than promote it. Ownership cannot be imposed through financial leverage and conditionality. Ownership would remain elusive until and unless there is a widespread acceptance of policies and political will among the country's political leadership and people at large. If imposed externally, it may fuel public discontent against donor agencies for their undue interference in the borrowing countries.

Judicial reform constitutes another important component of

current governance agenda where reforms have been introduced in a technocratic manner in diverse country settings. Not only is the agenda predominantly biased towards enforcement of private property rights and contracts, it disregards the complexities of legal and dispute settlement systems of the borrowing countries. After spending millions of dollars in projects related to judicial reforms, the Bank's intervention has failed to yield desired results. A survey on judicial reform and economic development published in the Bank's own journal called into question the actual impact of judicial reforms on economic development.[23] The sudden imposition of formal mechanisms to resolve disputes without understanding the specificities of the countries concerned is not an ideal solution. The IFIs have failed to realize that legal system, including those in the developed countries, takes decades and centuries to develop and therefore they cannot be implanted overnight. As rightly observed by Kapur and Webb, "Judicial reform illustrates several features of the way in which the IFIs have approached governance issues. One is a combination of impatience and a readiness to use borrowers as guinea pigs."[24]

Nowadays the international aid community gives more emphasis on decentralization and local self-governance (involving local bodies and NGOs in the developmental projects) in order to reduce poverty and achieve higher economic growth. To a large extent, the new shift towards involving local bodies and NGOs in aid projects has to do with the earlier disappointment with state-to-state development cooperation. The mushrooming of NGOs since the 1970s has also added impetus to this shift.[25] In the spirit of decentralization and local self-governance, essential developmental tasks are being handed over to local bodies and NGOs without examining their performance, capacity to deliver and sustainability. In India, for instance, the experiment with Panchayati Raj institutions (village level decentralized system of governance) shows that such initiatives, by and large, have not ushered a new era in participatory and accountable development. With few exceptions, Panchayat-run schools and other local services are as badly governed as the state-run ones. Since unequal power structures exist at local level, it would be erroneous to presume that such institutions should function impartially.

The accountability of NGOs remains open to question. There are NGOs which are more accountable to donors rather than to people they serve. Further, there are limits to which the NGOs can function effectively. Since NGOs lack the power and legitimacy to enforce their edict, most of their efforts remain voluntary, precisely because they cannot perform the functions of a legally constituted government. Attempts to promote decentralization are likely to fail until and unless they restructure power relations between government and local communities in a meaningful way.

Another dimension of good governance pertains to fostering popular participation. In reality, participation is increasingly being viewed as a technical issue, overlooking the fact that it is political in character. Viewed technically, participation, at best, is meant to ensure efficient implementation of policies without any meaningful say in the decision-making processes. The term 'participation' has been frequently used in several PRSPs. A survey of civil society's participation in the PRSPs in several countries reveals the poor levels of participation in the drawing up of PRSPs and I-PRSPs.[26] The survey found that the bulk of NGOs are disenchanted with the participation processes, as they were not adequately consulted in the preparation of these papers. Common problems expressed in the survey include lack of timely involvement, lack of information on macro-economic issues, exclusion from discussion on important matters such as strategies, and so forth.

The emphasis on financing education and health care through 'cost recovery' and 'prepayment schemes' is conspicuous in several PRSPs of Burkina Faso, Malawi, Mauritania, Rwanda, Uganda and Tanzania. However, this approach disregards the fact that poor people in these countries lack purchasing power to access these services and higher user-fees for health and education services would aggravate (not reduce) poverty. Withdrawal of state from public services could result in denying poor people access to basic services. The privatization of the Dar es Salaam Water and Sewerage Authority (DAWASA) under the HIPC debt relief initiative demonstrates how poor people could be excluded from an affordable clean water supply.

The governance agenda places special emphasis on anti-corruption measures. Under the new initiatives launched by the US and UK governments, aid would be given to only those countries that undertake anti-corruption measures. It needs to be recognized that corruption is a widespread phenomenon, not merely restricted to the poor and the developing world. The scale of corruption is global. Politicians of the developed world [from Vice-President Spiro Agnew (US) to Chancellor Helmut Kohl (Germany) to Prime Minister Noboru Takeshita (Japan)] have been accused of their involvement in corruption scandals. Not long ago, international financial institutions supported some of the worst corrupt regimes. The IMF and World Bank supported and sustained some of the notorious corrupt regimes for decades (for instance, Mobutu in Zaire and Duvalier in Haiti) despite being full aware that their aid money was not going to help the poor.

It is often the case that the solution to corruption is sought through reduction in the size of the government (in particular, downsizing of bureaucracy) by means of privatization and deregulation. Despite massive privatization of public sector enterprises and large-scale downsizing of bureaucracy in several poor and the developing countries, the level of corruption has not gone down. On the contrary, corruption has increased in several countries as privatization of public sector enterprises has given new opportunities for corruption. There are ample instances of privatization in Russia, India, Pakistan and a host of other countries where such deals were executed through corrupt methods. As noted by Harvey Feigenbaum and his colleagues, privatization should be considered as a political phenomenon rather than technical and economic response to increase the efficiency of state enterprises and institutions.[27]

Further, the exclusive focus on corruption in public offices and institutions fails to chronicle the large-scale corrupt practices carried out by private individuals and corporations. The involvement of Western banks and transnational corporations in many corrupt deals in the poor and the developing world is well documented. Notwithstanding the growing number of transnational corporations signing the OECD Convention against bribery, the level of corruption has not come down. The extent of corrupt practices involving transnational corporations is so huge that during 1994-2001, the US government received reports of 400 international contracts worth $200 billion that involved bribery. Ultimately, it is the people who pay the price of corruption through increased debts and overpriced projects and services provided by corporations.

The series of financial scandals in corporate America (from Enron to WorldCom) are instances of corruption by big corporations in connivance with other private parties such as fund managers, brokers, financiers, auditors and investment banks. These scandals have patently exposed the systemic flaws in the highly acclaimed American model of governance based on self-regulation.

Besides, these scandals have also demolished the popular myth that corruption is only limited to the public sector. Accountability and transparency issues are equally important for the private sector.

For good governance to be strengthened, the state must be made accountable and democratic. It is not the size of government that matters but the quality. The 'participatory budgeting' experiment in the city of Porto Alegre (Brazil) and the 'Kerala model' (India) are examples of active state involvement coupled with strong popular mobilization and engagement in the decision-making processes by labor unions, peasant organizations and popular movements. It is high time that the donor community, particularly the IFIs, recognizes the limits of development cooperation strategies which undermine the role of the state.

Politics Matters

The current narrow technocratic approaches to governance depoliticize foreign aid and development, converting it to a technical mechanism which could be evaluated by quantitative performance indicators. Although some analysts have argued that by taking up governance issues, the international aid community has shown interest in coming to terms with political dimensions of development. But by negating the issues of politics, power relations and special interest groups, the aid agencies (particularly the IFIs) have, so far, failed to visualize governance issues in a holistic perspective. Their resistance to admit that governance problems are political problems stems from their ideological moorings and a false notion of 'political neutrality' which delinks economic issues from politics. The technical approaches (irrespective of their technical and institutional soundness) are not sufficient in promoting good governance. Without addressing the underlying power relations in a given society, technical approaches such as training of judges, parliamentarians and civil servants would not lead to any meaningful contribution to governance issues. There is a need to steer away from the superficial boundaries of 'technocratic consensus' and start treating governance issues as political issues.

Put simply, politics matters. As rightly emphasized by Carlos Santiso, "Without addressing the underlying distribution of power, parliaments will likely remain passive and judiciaries dominated by the will of omnipotent executives. Although IFIs should not meddle in politics, they should not be politically naïve and cannot be oblivious of the political economy context. Governance reform and institutional development require focusing more explicitly and more rigorously on issues of power, politics and democracy."[28] According to Carlos, what is needed is a more radical approach in which donors cede developing countries greater control over the use of aid, within the framework of agreed-upon objectives.[29]

If the governance agenda has to succeed, there must be reciprocal institutional reforms both within the international aid community and borrower countries. Such an approach requires a wider vision that moves beyond 'compacts' like NEPAD. Further, it needs to be acknowledged that addressing political dimensions of development is not going to be an easy task as it fundamentally challenges the donors' interventions on governance issues and significantly the influence exercised by international power configurations.

Governance of IFIs: Good or Bad?

Although the IFIs — the World Bank and the IMF — relentlessly preach developing countries to improve their governance yet these institutions follow highly undemocratic structures and poor governance standards. Voting rights in the World Bank and IMF are still governed by the archaic rules framed in 1944. Although the reality of world economy has changed dramatically over the decades but voting rights of IFIs are governed by 1944 rules. No doubt, the membership of over 180 countries gives IFIs a multilateral character but unequal voting rights and faulty quota formula grant disproportionate power to a small number of developed countries to control these institutions.

What is even more disturbing to note is that a few developed member-countries (who do not borrow funds from these institutions) decide the lending conditions and other policy matters whereas the majority of member-countries of IFIs (who borrow funds from these institutions) hardly count in the decision-making structure. Take the case of IMF. The G-7 countries control nearly 47 per cent of total voting power in the IMF. If countries such as Belgium, Netherlands, Australia and Switzerland are added, the developed ones can determine final outcome on vital issues that require a simple majority of total votes in the IMF. Similar is the problem with the World Bank's governing structure.

The imbalance in voting rights ensures inadequate representation of the poor and the developing countries in the Executive Boards of the IFIs. Only a handful of developing countries such as Brazil, China and India have their own representatives in the Executive Boards of the IFIs. The rest have their representatives by rotations or they join a large regional grouping. For instance, the voting rights of 21 Sub-Saharan African countries (3.2 per cent of the total votes) are so small that they have just one Executive Director in the 24-member Executive Board of IMF. One would expect the disproportionate voting shares of developed countries would lead to greater responsibility and accountability on their part. On the contrary, there are several instances where the developed countries have increased their power and influence without contributing additional funds to the IFIs.[30]

Further, the rapid increase in the numbers of decisions that require qualified majorities has led to such a situation where one country (US with 17 per cent votes) or a small group of five developed countries can veto any proposal concerning amendments of the Charters, distribution of capital and allocation of SDRs.

The IFIs still follow another unwritten archaic rule under which the President of the World Bank is the nominee of the US while an European nominee heads the IMF. In other words, it is the nationality that guides the selection rather than merit. Time and again, developed countries have deliberately marginalized the role of developing countries in the selection process of the Managing Director of the Bank and the IMF. The selection process is determined by closed-door informal negotiations between the US and Europe. With over 70 percent professional staff belonging to Europe and North America, there is predominance of developed countries in the staff of the IFIs.

Under their Articles of Agreement, both the Bank and the IMF are not supposed to enter into policy conditionality and restructuring of the economy of the member-countries. But both institutions have expanded their policy conditionality over the years. As discussed earlier, not only the number of conditionalities has increased but also their scope has widened beyond core monetary and fiscal macroeconomic issues. Now with the incorporation of governance reforms, the mandate of the IFIs has been further widened. Despite large-scale expansion in their operations, IFIs are yet to make any meaningful headway on the accountability front. The IFIs remain secretive and unaccountable. Under strong pressure generated by civil society, the IFIs have undertaken measly reforms in the last few years in terms of transparency and consultation. Yet these reforms are not adequate for ensuring wider accountability, both vertical (staff to Executive Board) and horizontal. Recent efforts to instill accountability (such as World Bank Inspection Panel, IFC Ombudsman, Independent Evaluation Office, etc.) are more of a public relation exercise than any genuine concern for accountability since these establishments lack enforcement powers.

The lack of transparency and good governance norms at the IFIs not only makes a mockery of tall claims, but more importantly, questions their legitimacy and authority as the institutions of global governance.

Time to Broaden the Discourse on Good Governance

Given the fact that the dominant discourse on good governance is increasingly becoming superficial and constricted with sole emphasis on state institutions and structures, the time has come to broaden the concept to include all formal and informal actors who play a role in decision-making or in influencing the decision-making process. Viewed in totality, the notion of governance would also encompass all non-state actors including markets and civil society. Therefore, it stands to reason that governance issues should also be addressed to the corporate world, financial markets, multilateral financial institutions, multilateral trade bodies, bilateral donor agencies, media, religious groups, political parties, NGOs, trade unions, etc.

In the new global setting, corporate governance issues need far greater attention than ever since corporate globalization unleashes forces with little public accountability. There are over 63000 parent TNCs with over 800000 foreign subsidiaries. Besides, corporations are increasingly taking control of industries and services previously run by governments, without shouldering public responsibilities. The 1984 accident at Union Carbide's factory in Bhopal (India), in which 6000 people were killed and over 150000 suffered grievous ailments, is a grim reminder that exempting the corporate world from the purview of governance and accountability could lead to large-scale human and environmental catastrophe. The Bhopal disaster is also one of the examples of the double standards displayed by the TNCs regarding consumer protection, environmental and employment concerns in their home and host countries.

Studies have pointed out that TNCs often form trade cartels and indulge in manipulative transfer pricing causing substantial loss of tax revenue and foreign exchange to the poor and the developing world. Although anti-corporate activists have been demanding wider corporate accountability for decades, corporate governance was never on the agenda of international financial institutions, powerful states and corporate entities.

It is only in the aftermath of a series of financial scandals that rocked corporate America in 2002 that the issues of corporate governance came into prominence in the international policy circles. Despite much-touted claims of corporate transparency and disclosures, the basic norms of governance were completely flouted in all these scams. The corporate governance problem is so widespread that almost 1000 American corporations have restated their earnings since 1997. Notwithstanding the regulations laid down by the US regulatory authority, Securities and Exchange Commission (SEC), almost every big American corporation had its corporate code of ethics. Though it is a different matter that they repeatedly violated their own codes. These unsavory episodes have put a serious question mark on the relevance of code of ethics. It has also patently exposed the systemic flaws in the highly acclaimed American model of governance based on self-regulation.

Concluding Remarks

By limiting the concept of good governance to technical mechanisms which could be evaluated by qualitative performance indicators, wider issues such as control over wealth and power, domination by TNCs and finance capital, the influence of IFIs and WTO, and inequalities and asymmetries within and among nations are not being addressed as issues of governance.

For the vast majority of people, good governance also means a better quality of life; an equitable distribution of wealth, income and natural resources; dismantling of highly concentrated structures of property ownership; full employment; access to housing, health and education; restraining privileges of elites; the right to choose alternatives; cultural development and so on so forth. A good governance system is the one under which all public policy affairs are managed through broad consensus in a transparent, accountable, participatory and equitable manner. Such an ideal system of good governance remains a far cry in the developed world, leave alone the poor and the developing world.

Good governance cannot be an end in itself. It is an evolving process and has the potential to become a potent instrument for radical transformation provided it is applied in all spheres of social life. Like democracy, good governance cannot be implanted or imposed by the donor community, it has to be imbibed, nurtured and cherished from within.

Notes and References

1. *The Economic Times*, December 17, 2002, p. 7.

2. It is important to stress here that the World Bank is not the only multi-lateral aid agency promoting good governance. Other important multi-lateral and regional developmental agencies actively promoting governance issues include ADB, IMF, UNDP, OECD, EBRD, etc. For instance, the Asian Development Bank was the first regional development bank which adopted an official 'governance' policy in 1995. In addition, a host of bilateral donors [for instance, the US Agency for International Development (USAID), the British Department for International Development (DFID) and the Swedish International Development Cooperation Agency (SIDA)] spend millions of dollars each year to support governance related programs in several developing countries. Many of these bilateral donors have also constituted special units to coordinate their governance-related activities. Unfortunately, the governance agenda of bilateral donors continues to be set by the IFIs. Private foundations are also not lagging behind. For instance, the Open Society, founded by financier, George Soros, is actively promoting democracy and governance related projects in Central and Eastern Europe.

3. Some analysts have offered plausible economic and political reasons for the use of term 'governance' instead of government. According to Sophal Ear, a former World Bank official, "the phenomenal rise of governance as opposed to government, in a normative context, may also have a great deal to do with its more palatable sound — to say "bad government" to a Prime Minister is akin to telling him he is a "bad" person. While to say that his government suffers from bad governance sounds more diplo-matic — and international financial institutions (IFIs) like the World Bank and the IMF are, if nothing else, diplomatic organizations."

4. Daniel Kaufmann, Aart Kraay and Pablo Zoido-Lobaton, "Aggregating Governance Indicators," *Policy Research Working Paper*, No. 2195, World Bank, Washington D.C., October 1999; and Daniel Kaufmann, Aart Kraay, and Pablo Zoido-Lobaton, "Governance Matters," *Policy Research Working Paper*, No. 2196, World Bank, Washington D.C., October 1999.

5. The history of quantitative measures of governance dates back to 1955 when a US-based foundation, Freedom House, published a report, *Freedom in the World*, which covered political rights, civil liberties, and free-dom of the press. The foundation publishes this report every year. Cur-rently, an international NGO, Transparency International, is also bring-ing out a Corruption Perception Index which deals with corruption and

public sector reforms. Besides, a number of bilateral donors have published handbooks and issued guidelines on governance indicators.

6. The IMF and the World Bank in their Annual Meetings embarked on PRSPs in September 1999. They replaced structural adjustment programs as the new pre-condition for loans and debt relief. The Enhanced Structural Adjustment Facility (ESAF) of IMF has been replaced by the Poverty Reduction and Growth Facility (PRGF), and the PRSPs have become an integral component of the HIPC initiative and a precondition for access to the Poverty Reduction Support Credit (PRSC) introduced by the World Bank in 2001. PRSPs have now become a condition for most development aid to the world's poorest countries. The IFIs have also pushed other donors (for instance, European Union) to link their aid to Poverty Reduction Strategies. PRSPs were supposed to mark a major shift. Borrowing countries were to design their own development strategies, and these were to be more explicitly focused on poverty reduction. Besides the involvement of IFIs, borrowing countries were supposed to seek broader participation of civil society and other stakeholders in the preparation of I-PRSPs (Interim PRSPs) and PRSPs. However, in reality, PRSPs are not different from earlier structural adjustment programs as their core economic elements consist of deregulation, privatization, liberalization and rolling back of state. Critics have also pointed out that borrowing countries write into the PRSPs what would be acceptable to the donors.

7. George W. Bush, "Remarks by the President at United Nations Financing for Development Conference, Monterrey, Mexico," March 22, 2002.

8. NEPAD is based on the concept of mutual accountability and calls for a new 'compact' between African countries and external donors. It calls for African countries to undertake drastic political and economic reforms and in return, external donors would provide aid, debt relief and market access.

9. The term 'Washington Consensus' was first coined by the US economist John Williamson to refer to policy package pushed by the powerful Washington-based institutions, namely, the World Bank, IMF, the US Treasury and neoliberal think-tanks. Initially aimed at Latin American countries in the 1980s, Washington Consensus was subsequently extended to the rest of the developing world. The important components of the Washington Consensus were fiscal discipline; trade liberalization; tax reforms; liberalization of foreign investment regime; privatization; deregulation; financial liberalization and capital account liberalization; market-based exchange rate; labor reforms; and protection of property rights.

10. A US-based economist, Dani Rodrik, has examined this issue in an institutionalized context. See Dani Rodrik, "Institutions for High-Quality Growth: What They Are and How to Acquire Them?," paper presented at the IMF Conference on Second Generation Reforms, Washington D.C., November 8-9, 1999; and Dani Rodrik, "After Neoliberalism, What?," in *After Neoliberalism: Economic Policies that Work for the Poor*, New Rules for Global Finance Coalition, Washington D.C., October 2002.

11. UNCTAD, *From Adjustment to Poverty Reduction: What is New?*, New York and Geneva, 2002, p. 6.

12. Development Committee, "Note from the President of the World Bank," Prague, September 18, 2000, p. 4.

13. Devesh Kapur and Richard Webb, *Governance-Related Conditionalities of the International Financial Institutions*, UNCTAD, G-24 Discussion Paper Series 6, UNCTAD, New York and Geneva, 2000, p. 4.

14. Ibid.

15. Ibid.

16. There is an ongoing debate about the proper demarcation of responsibilities between the IMF and the World Bank, popularly known as 'mission creep,' because of the Bank's involvement in governance issues and IMF's involvement in poverty reduction programs have led to significant encroachment on each other's traditional institutional turfs. In addition, since governance issues are political issues, these fall outside the mandate of the IFIs as their founding charters prohibit political considerations in designing the aid programs.

17. Carlos Santiso, "Good Governance and Aid Effectiveness: The World Bank and Conditionality," *The Georgetown Public Policy Review*, Vol. 7, Number 1, Fall 2001, pp. 1-23; and Carlos Santiso, "International Cooperation for Democracy and Good Governance," *European Journal of Development Research*, Vol. 13, Number 1, 2001, pp. 154-180.

18. Paul Mosley, Jane Harrigan and John Toye (eds.), *Aid and Power: The World Bank and Policy-based Lending*, Routledge, London, 1991.

19. Shantayanan Devarajan, David Dollar and Torgny Holgren, *Aid and Reform in Africa: Lessons from Ten Case Studies*, World Bank, Washington D.C., 2001.

20. Tony Killick, *Aid and the Political Economy of Policy Change*, Overseas Development Institute, London, 1998.

21. Stephen Knack, "Aid Dependence and the Quality of Governance: A

Cross-Country Empirical Analysis," *Policy Research Working Paper*, No. 2396, World Bank, Washington D.C., July 2000.

22. UNCTAD, op.cit., p. 58.

23. R. E. Messick, "Judicial Reform and Economic Development: A Survey of the Issues," *The World Bank Research Observer*, Vol. 14, No. 1, February 1999, pp. 117-136.

24. Devesh Kapur and Richard Webb, op.cit., p. 11.

25. It needs to be stressed here that international aid agencies particularly encourage only those NGOs, community groups and local bodies which are ideologically inclined towards market reforms and liberal democracy.

26. World Development Movement, *Policies to Roll Back the State and Privatise?*, London, April 2001.

27. For details, see Harvey Feigenbaum, Jeffrey Henig and Chris Hamnett, *Shrinking the State: The Political Underpinnings of Privatization*, Cambridge University Press, Cambridge, 1998.

28. Carlos Santiso, *Governance Conditionality and the Reform of Multilateral Development Finance: The Role of the Group of Eight*, G8 Governance, Number 7, 2002, p. 29.

29. Carlos Santiso, op.cit. Fall 2001, p. 19.

30. For details, see, Devesh Kapur, *Do As I Say Not As I Do: A Critique of G-7 Proposals on Reforming the Multilateral Development Banks*, G-24 Discussion Paper Series No. 20, February 2003; and Aziz Ali Mohammed, "The Democratic Deficit in International Decision Making: A Developing Country Perspective," Remarks at The Challenge of Global Democracy: An NGO Retreat Addressing the Democratic Deficit in International Decision Making, Washington D.C., December 4, 2003.

CHAPTER 5

Does Globalization Spell the End of Nation-State?

The nation state has rapidly become an unnatural, even dysfunctional, unit in terms of which to think about or organize economic activity...Nation states are dinosaurs waiting to die.

Kenichi Ohmae

MANY commentators are of the viewpoint that the ascendancy of globalization leads to the demise of nation-state.[1] It is claimed that globalization processes are creating a truly 'global' economy dominated by transnational corporations and financial markets in which political boundaries are no longer relevant. Further, it is asserted that economies have been integrated in global economy in such a manner that national level policy solutions have become obsolete. Not only hyper-globalists, even some well meaning anti-globalists also share similar false notions. Such a superficial understanding fails to capture the essence of the complex relationship between globalization and nation-state. There is no denying that the growing domination of transnational capital in various forms poses new challenges to pursue independent economic policy making and promote redistributive policies but it would be off the mark to conclude that the nation-state would wither away or become irrelevant.

If globalization was perceived to destroy nation-states, then it has completely failed to do so. Far from vanishing, several new states have been formed in the past two decades and many more could be expected in the times to come. At present, there are 192 independent nation-states, compared to just 70 in 1946.

In contrast to the claims made by the hyper-globalists, borders still matter. There are very few regions in the world where border disputes have altogether disappeared. Regardless of its geographical location, private capital (domestic or transnational) operates within a particular national jurisdiction.

Those who augur the demise of the nation-state under the impact of globalization simply ignore the fact that political power still resides in the arena of nation-state and pressures generated by national social and political institutions and interest groups shape the final policy outcomes. Unlike states, transnational capital lacks sovereign power to enforce its agenda.

How Global is Globalization?

Contrary to neoliberal presumptions, the contemporary world economy is far from being truly 'global.' Bulk of trade, production and financial flows are still concentrated in a handful of developed countries. The following facts corroborate the viewpoint that globalization is by no means a truly 'global' and even process:

■ FDI flows are highly concentrated and unevenly distributed around the world. Although FDI flows have increased in developing countries, over two-thirds of flows are concentrated among the members of the Triad — the US, EU and Japan.

■ Around 90 per cent of the world's top 100 non-financial TNCs are headquartered in the Triad.

■ There are very few truly stateless 'global' TNCs. There is no denying that in an era of declining constraints on capital mobility and the attraction of low wages in the developing countries, TNCs are shifting production abroad. But only low value, labor-intensive activities are being shifted to the developing countries while strategic operations such as research and development (R&D), headquarters and financial management continue to be located in the home country. Besides, the board of directors and senior management personnel predominantly belong to the home country. A large majority of shareholders also belong to the home country. Even in instances where globalization of strategic operations such as R&D has taken place, it has remained a regional phenomenon.

■ Over 85 per cent of production in the developed countries is for the domestic market.

■ With few exceptions, transnational corporations are still dependent on home markets. Take the case of international banks. Despite considerable acquisition of assets abroad, most international banks' assets still remain in their domestic markets. To illustrate, Citigroup with operations in more than 100 countries cannot be portrayed as a truly 'global' bank because the bulk of its assets are in the US. With only 34 per cent of assets held outside the US, Citigroup is essentially a domestic US bank. Just 30 banks worldwide have more than one-third of their total assets outside their domestic markets.

■ Instead of becoming stateless 'global' enterprises, most TNCs are deeply rooted in their national societies and maintain their distinct social, economic, and political value systems. Paul Doremus and his colleagues in their book, *The Myth of the Global Corporation*, have unveiled how American, German and Japanese transnational corporations are embedded in the history, culture, and economic systems of their respective home societies.[2]

■ Most TNCs maintain close ties with their home country governments.

■ Much of international trade of goods and services is intra-regional (particularly in Europe and North America), rather than inter-regional.

It also needs to be noted that trade, investment and capital flows are not much higher nowadays than the earlier phase of globalization.[3] During the *Belle Epoque* period from 1870 to 1913, the world economy was highly integrated with massive cross-border movement of goods, capital and people. The trade-GDP ratio of several developed countries was as significant as the present times. Japan's trade-GDP ratio was actually higher than the present times. In UK, trade-GDP ratio stood at 44 per cent in 1910, as compared to 57 per cent in 1995. While in the case of Germany, it was 46 per cent against 38 per cent in the same period. In the earlier period, the UK had substantial cross-border capital investments, averaging 4.6 per cent of GDP. At that time, much of private capital flowed into bonds to finance railways, roads and other infrastructure projects. The world financial system, at that time, ran according to the rules of the Classical Gold Standard.

Unlike the present phase of globalization, international labor migration was mammoth during that period, as there was no restrictions on the movement of people across borders. Nowadays immigration controls are much tighter than ever.

Have States become Powerless and Obsolete?

The much-touted claim that states have become powerless and obsolete in the wake of contemporary globalization is grounded on false assumptions. First, not all states have become powerless under the influence of transnational capital as there are significant variations across countries. As noted by Ha-Joon Chang, the influence of transnational capital on individual states is highly uneven and varies from issue to issue.[4] The degree of influence is largely dependent on the size, military strength and power of states. Admittedly, the globalization processes may have weakened the bargaining powers of smaller and weaker states but there are hardly any examples where the entire state structures have collapsed for prolonged period. Even in certain African countries where the collapse of state structures is somewhat evident, the collapse had more to do with the domestic social and political reasons. On the other hand, powerful states (for instance, US) still retain considerable clout to pursue domestic and international policies suiting their national interests.

It is not always that transnational capital enjoys an upper hand in bargaining. Countries with a large domestic market (for instance, China and India) can bargain better terms and conditions from transnational capital, than the ones with small domestic market (for instance, Bangladesh and Ethiopia). Further, the bargaining power is determined by the nature of industries. Unlike mining and forestry where production sites are very limited, transnational capital holds greater bargaining power in industries such as garments and toys due to abundance of alternative sites.[5]

The national policy response to globalization processes also varies across countries. For instance, some governments have allowed complete takeover of domestic assets by transnational capital while other governments have forced mergers and acquisitions among domestic entities to ensure that they can effectively compete with transnational capital. Besides, there are several instances where governments, particularly those belonging to the developed world, have resorted to protectionist measures to safeguard domestic economic sectors.

Second, the budgets of governments have not diminished with the adoption of open economy. In most highly integrated countries, government spending is increasing, rather than declining. Government spending accounts as much as half of their national income in many developed countries. As rightly pointed out by Dani Rodrik, the more open the economy, the more is the need for state intervention to assist those adversely affected by globalization.[6]

Third, privatization of public sector enterprises does not necessarily mean overall decline in state intervention in the economy. Privatization may lead to a decline in the public ownership but there might be an increase in the state regulation through the establishment of regulatory authority, competition policy, disclosure norms and other new policy measures. In this regard, Harvey Feigenbaum and his colleagues in their book, *Shrinking the State*, have examined the large-scale privatization program of Margaret Thatcher government in the UK.[7] According to them, the privatization program under Thatcher government led to the reduction of the role of government in the direct provisions of the services such as telephone, electricity and water but the country simultaneously witnessed the emergence of new regulatory authorities with enormous powers to ensure that privatized utilities should not exploit consumers. As a result, there was no reduction in state intervention in totality.

Fourth, it is likely that the role of the state may reduce in certain sectors of economy but it may expand significantly elsewhere. Similarly, the repressive powers of the governments may also expand. In the wake of globalization, the repressive powers of many states have expanded rather than shrinking. Increasingly, states are taking recourse to anti-democratic methods to suppress social and political movements seeking genuine democratization. There have been several instances (e.g., Shell in Nigeria and mass protests against adjustment programs in Mexico, Argentina, Venezuela and Indonesia) where the governments took to repressive measures against their own people in order to protect the interests of transnational capital. The rise in repressive measures in the name of preserving 'law and order' and maintaining a favorable investment climate has grave implications for the human rights (particularly economic and social rights) of vast majority of people. In the developed world too, repressive powers are increasing. In the aftermath of September 11, 2001 attacks, the Bush administration enacted several draconian laws to curb democratic freedom and rights. Many other countries have imposed similar repressive measures too.

Lastly, the term deregulation could be misleading as semantically it means re-regulation. For instance, the captains of global capital demand strong regulation of trade union activity while insisting on complete deregulation of wages and labor markets.

Can Globalization Survive without Nation-States?

As propagated, globalization is neither a natural nor an autonomous phenomenon. Rather it has been shaped by the complex and dynamic set of interactions between transnational capital and nation-states. The present phase of globalization could not have proceeded without the active participation of states through liberalization of trade, foreign investment and industrial policies. A favorable international political environment created and sustained by certain powerful states, particularly the US, played a crucial role in the aggrandizement of transnational capital in the post-World War II era.

In contrast to the popular perception, states play an indispensable role in the advancement and sustenance of contemporary globalization. The world economy is still governed by nation-states, along with several inter-state institutional arrangements created and sustained by them. Undoubtedly the character of the state has changed profoundly over the years but the state and inter-state institutional arrangements manage and steer contemporary world economy. The role of certain powerful states in shaping the contours of contemporary world economy is well recognized.

On its own, transnational capital lacks the necessary power and ability to mould the world economy in its favor. Rather, it strives for the support of nation-states and inter-state institutions to shape the contemporary world economy.[8] Undeniably, financial markets have become powerful with trillions of dollars moving across the borders daily but cross-border movement of funds was primarily made possible by the removal of capital controls by governments (willingly or unwillingly) since the mid-1970s.

In the global capitalism context, nation-states provide the framework within which all markets operate. The notion of 'free market' is a myth as all markets are governed by regulations. Though the nature and degree of regulation may vary from market to market. Even the much-claimed self-regulation model would be illegitimate if it is not backed by the government decree. In fact, it is impossible to conceive contemporary globalization without laws, and laws do not exist outside the realm of nation-states. Even the global rules on trade and investment enforced by international institutions (for instance, WTO) are not independent of nation-states.

State policies are vital for the advancement and sustenance of transnational capital on a world scale. Investment decisions by

Kavaljit Singh

transnational capital are not always influenced by the degree of liberalization but are governed by state regulations in areas as diverse as taxation, trade, investment, currency, property rights and labor. A stable economic and political environment is also one of the important determinants. Transnational capital looks upon legislative, judicial and executive institutions to not merely protect and enforce property rights and contract laws but also to provide social, political, and macroeconomic stability. In the absence of such policy framework, contemporary globalization would not have taken place. Social and political conflicts are also resolved primarily through state mechanisms. The fact that strong and stable state is a prerequisite for the development and sustenance of market economy is evident from the failure of economic reforms in transition countries.

In addition, state intervention is also necessary to prevent and correct market failures. There are innumerable instances of market failures with huge social costs throughout the world. Although all markets are imperfect and liable to fail, financial markets are more prone to failure because of asymmetric information, herd behavior and self-fulfilling panics.[9] These factors make financial markets more inefficient and volatile. Due to its speculative behavior, finance capital would collapse on its own in the absence of state regulations.

Corporate world relies on state apparatus for providing financial stability. Majority of TNCs will suffer losses if the volatility in exchange rates is not tamed by international policy coordination. On numerous occasions, powerful states have coordinated their policies and deliberately intervened in the foreign exchange markets to bring financial stability. For instance, the Plaza and Louvre Accords among the G-7 countries in the 1980s were attempts to establish greater international currency stability. In the aftermath of Southeast Asian financial crisis, countries from the region have coordinated their policies and launched regional arrangements such as Asian Bond Fund and currency swap agreements to protect their economies from volatile capital flows. In 1997, Japan also proposed the establishment of an Asian Monetary Fund to address regional monetary issues.

Private capital (domestic or transnational) still relies on state resources in several areas, particularly physical infrastructure such as roads, railways, airports, seaports and telecommunications. In addition, it also relies on state resources for providing human infrastructure (educated workforce), research and development, tax concessions as well as direct financial support. The tax concessions and huge subsidies to Boeing Corporation and Airbus Industries are shining examples of financial support to big corporations. In the aftermath of the attacks on the World Trade Center and Pentagon on September 11, 2001, the US administration approved $15 billion bailout package for the airline industry. While over 500000 employees who lost their jobs in the wake of attacks on the World Trade Center did not receive any financial support.

Leave aside the developing world, even in the US, federal government played a catalytic role in the country's development. The federal government established telecommunications by funding the first telegraph line between Baltimore and Washington in 1842. In the twentieth century, much of America's technological advancement was made possible by government-funded research programs. The predominant role of government-funded research institutions and universities (e.g., National Institute of Health) in the initiation of basic research for the development of several drugs is well recognized. Through a combination of policy measures including research funding and strong enforcement of intellectual property rights, the US government has been sustaining an enabling environment for the advancement of R&D in new fields such as biotechnology. Internet is another illustration of the government support for the development of new technologies. It was the Pentagon that initially developed the enabling technology of Internet for military purposes, via APRA-net. In the same vein, the federal government aided advancement in aviation sector.

In the case of India too, its growing international presence in the computer, biotechnology and other high technology sectors has been made possible by the government-funded research institutes such as Indian Institutes of Technology. All these examples show beyond doubt that the state is actively involved in the advancement of economic globalization processes.

While arguing that the globalization processes are deeply embedded with the state, one is not negating the existence of conflicts between transnational capital and states. Since the *raison d'être* of these two entities are different, conflicts are unlikely to disappear. As opposed to transnational capital with its single-minded pursuit of profit maximization, national governments have to carry out diverse economic, social and political tasks to meet the needs of their citizens. These conflicts would persist as victims of globalization look upon the state institutions to provide them economic and social security.

International Institutional Arrangements and Globalization

Since 1945, the world has witnessed a plethora of international institutional arrangements. In addition, a large number of declarations, conventions and treaties in economic and political affairs have been signed by nation-states. International institutional arrangements including the EU, UN, NATO, IMF, World Bank, WTO, OECD and Bank for International Settlement are not independent entities but have been created and nurtured by nation-states. The World Bank and the IMF, for instance, are not controlled by private financiers and large transnational banks but by a handful of creditor states.

Inter-state institutional arrangements are essentially governed by the balance of power among member-countries. Due to unequal power relations, certain powerful states exert considerable influence in deciding the policy framework of these institutions. The US, in particular, has had a decisive say in determining the policy agenda of many institutional arrangements. The US domination of multilateral financial institutions such as the World Bank and the IMF is well known. It is also a well-established fact that the EU and US enjoy a disproportionate influence on the agenda of global trade regime enforced by the WTO. Within the highly integrated EU, the influence of certain powerful states such as Germany, UK and France has not diminished despite 10 new countries joined it in 2004.

The inter-state institutional arrangements — in particular multilateral financial institutions, bilateral and multilateral trade agreements and regional groupings — played a catalyzing role in pushing ahead the liberalization and globalization agenda. As delineated elsewhere in this book, several instruments and institutions were used to facilitate this process on a world scale, particularly to open up the economies of the developing and transition countries. The structural adjustment programs with rigid conditionalities were used to open up those countries experiencing balance of payments (BoP) or debt crises. While bilateral and multilateral trade agreements and treaties became the instruments to open up those economies not experiencing BoP or debt problems.

Nevertheless, it needs to be underscored that the growing influence of inter-state institutions such as IMF, World Bank and

WTO has not completely put an end to domestic economic policy making by the national governments. Irrespective of the degree of globalization, the role of nation-state would remain paramount in performing several functions including regulation and supervision of markets; social cohesion and political stability; and guarantor of the rule of the law.

Is Globalization Irreversible?

The oft-repeated assertion that political processes cannot reverse the march towards economic globalization is more a myth than reality. Economic globalization has been reversed by domestic political processes in the past and therefore could be reversed in the future. All public policies are the products of pressures generated by social and political institutions in a given society and are liable to change. If labor-friendly policies could be reversed to serve the interests of private capital, investor-friendly policies could also face the same fate.

There is nothing sacrosanct about the economic globalization processes. History is replete with instances where the pendulum had swung in the opposite direction due to unanticipated events. The advancement of earlier phase of globalization was scuttled by a series of events including World War I, the Great Depression and World War II. Whether the contemporary phase of globalization would face the same fate by such unforeseen events remains open to question.

In contrast to popular presumptions, there are alternatives. Nevertheless, it is the wider national and international context that determines the choice of particular policy alternatives. Within the present global capitalism context, a strategy calling for complete delinking of domestic economy from world economy or autarky may not succeed. While a strategy based on curbing unbridled financial liberalization and selective delinking from speculative funds is likely to succeed. There have been several attempts by countries to resist short-term, speculative financial flows in the late 1990s. The experiences of countries such as Malaysia, Chile and China show that selective delinking is not only desirable but also feasible. The terms and conditions of linkages with global financial flows should be decided democratically by people rather than by international financial institutions and private investors. If peoples' movements are strong, alert and influential, there is every possibility of devising an investment strategy which allows only such financial flows that are beneficial to the domestic economy. This does not mean that countries should blindly attract long-term FDI and other types of financial flows. As discussed in Chapter 2, the cost of FDI flows can be debilitating as capital can move out through royalty payments, dividends, imports as well as other legal and illegal means.

Delinking from speculative financial flows could be followed by alterating trade and investment agreements which disproportionately benefit transnational capital. The alternative development strategy should include enlarging the rights of governments over transnational capital through policy measures such as tough competitive laws, increased corporate taxes, capital controls, taxes on speculative investments, and stricter labor and environmental regulations.

Subordination of transnational capital to democratic controls could be supplemented by a fundamental reorientation of the domestic economy. The domestic economy should be restructured to serve the needs of those sections of society, which have been marginalized by both the state and the market forces. Growth must emanate primarily from domestic savings and investments. A progressive direct taxation system could enhance domestic financial resources. Rather than focusing on export-led growth, domestic markets should act as the prime engines of growth. Besides, the principle of equity must be given top priority by the governments.

However, fundamental reorientation of domestic economy is not viable without democratization of state and domestic arrangements of political power. In other words, a democratic and accountable state can act as a bulwark against the present trajectory of globalization besides broadening the space for alternative developmental strategy.

Globalization, Ethnicity and Nation-State

Over the years, nation-states have increasingly come under attack from ethnic nationalism. There is *per se* nothing wrong with the assertion of ethnic identity but it becomes a serious problem when ethnicity based on chauvinistic agenda is politicized to capture power and unleash a reign of terror against other ethnic groups. In many parts of the world, fundamentalist movements based on ethnic, religious or linguistic identities are challenging the integrity of existing states in several ways. Some ethnic movements are demanding greater autonomy while others are seeking complete independence. Diverse forms of fundamentalist movements and ethnic conflicts have mushroomed in Europe, Latin America, Africa and Asia. Though majority of ethnic conflicts and civil wars are located in the poorest regions of the world. Ethnic conflicts in Indonesia, Rwanda, Somalia and Sudan are examples of this phenomenon.

Escalation in the frequency of ethnic conflicts could be gauged from the alarming rise in the scale of civil wars in the 1990s. In this decade, most wars were fought on ethnic rather than on ideological grounds. In the late 1980s and early 1990s, formation of new states based on ethnicity witnessed a sharp rise and over 20 new states were formed after the collapse of USSR and Yugoslavia. Since then, several new states have been formed and many more are expected in the future.

The detailed analysis of causes behind the rise of ethnic nationalism is beyond the scope of this book. The linkages between globalization processes and the rise of ethnic nationalism are noticeable. But it would be an exaggeration to attribute the rise of ethnicity entirely to economic globalization processes since many fundamentalist movements existed even before the onset of present phase of globalization.

A closer examination of several ethnic conflicts reveals that these often originate due to unequal distribution of wealth and power. Massive job losses and unemployment due to global economic restructuring has exacerbated economic inequalities and social unrest. These conditions, in turn, create an atmosphere in which security and identities are perceived to be under threat. With the decline of class-based politics, fundamentalist movements have been successful in mobilizing the losers from globalization processes on the basis of ethnic, religious or national identity. It comes as no surprise that the social base of fundamentalist movements largely consists of the poor and disadvantaged groups who join these movements to regain their lost identity and economic stability through the capture of state power. Yet it needs to be noted that ethnic movements are not seeking complete collapse of nation-states rather they wish to create new nation-states based on their own ethnic identities.

Concluding Remarks

The world economy is still governed by nation-states, along with several inter-state institutional arrangements created and sustained by them. States have played an indispensable role in the advancement and sustenance of contemporary globalization. On its own, transnational capital cannot mould the world economy in its favor. Rather, it strives for the support of nation-states and inter-state institutions to shape the contemporary world economy.

No denying that contemporary economic globalization poses new challenges to national authorities but it would be erroneous to conclude that the nation-states would cease to exist. Despite global integration coupled with multi-layered apparatus of governance, the state will remain a key player in both domestic and international economic affairs.

Notes and References

1. Kenichi Ohmae is an ardent supporter of this thesis. For detailed account of his arguments, see Kenichi Ohmae, *The Borderless World*, Collins, London, 1990; and Kenichi Ohmae, *The End of the Nation State*, Free Press, New York, 1995.

2. For details, see Paul N. Doremus, William W. Keller, Louis W. Pauly and Simon Reich, *The Myth of the Global Corporation*, Princeton University Press, Princeton, 1998.

3. For a detailed account of earlier phase of globalization, see Paul Hirst and Grahame Thompson, "Globalization: Ten Frequently Asked Questions and Some Surprising Answers," *Soundings*, 4, 1996; Paul Hirst and Grahame Thompson, *Globalization in Question: The International Economy and the Possibilities of Governance*, Polity Press, Cambridge, 1996; Paul Hirst, "The Global Economy: Myths and Realities," *International Affairs*, No. 73, 1997; and David Held and Anthony McGrew, *Global Transformation*, Polity Press, Cambridge, 1999.

4. For details, see Ha-Joon Chang, *Globalisation, Economic Development and the Role of the State*, Zed Books, London and New York, 2003.

5. Ibid., p. 11.

6. For details, see Dani Rodrik, *Has Globalization Gone Too Far?*, Institute for International Economics, Washington D.C., 1997.

7. Harvey Feigenbaum, Jeffrey Henig and Chris Hamnett, *Shrinking the State: The Political Underpinnings of Privatization*, Cambridge University Press, Cambridge, 1998.

8. The role of nation-state in shaping and nurturing contemporary phase of globalization has been well-documented by several analysts. In particular see, Eric Helleiner, *States and the Re-emergence of Global Finance*, Cornell University Press, Ithaca, 1994; Saskia Sassen, *Losing Control? Sovereignty in an Age of Globalization*, Columbia University Press, New York, 1996; Samir Amin, *Capitalism in the Age of Globalization*, Madhyam Books, Delhi, 1997; Peter Dicken, *Global Shift*, Chapman, London, 1998; Linda Weiss, *The Myth of the Powerless State: Governing the Economy in a Global Era*, Polity Press, Cambridge, 1998; John Gray, *False Dawn*, Granta, London, 1998; Boris Kagarlitsky, *The Twilight of Globalization: Property, State and Capitalism*, Pluto Press, London, 2000; Noam Chomsky, *Profit Over People: Neoliberalism and Global Order*, Madhyam Books, Delhi, 1999; and James Petras and Henry Veltmeyer, *Globalization Unmasked: Imperialism in the 21st Century*, Madhyam Books, Delhi, 2001.

9. For detailed information on the failures of financial markets and financial crises, see Kavaljit Singh, *Taming Global Financial Flows: Challenges and Alternatives in the Era of Financial Globalization*, Zed Books, London, 2000.

Bibliography

Armijo, Leslie Elliott, *Financial Globalization and Democracy in Emerging Markets*, Macmillan Press Ltd., London, 1999.

Blum, William, *Rogue State: A Guide to the World's Only Superpower*, Zed Books, London, 2003.

Boggs, Carl, *The End of Politics: Corporate Power and the Decline of the Public Sphere*, The Guilford Press, London, 2000.

Chang, Ha-Joon, *Kicking Away the Ladder: Development Strategy in Historical Perspective*, Anthem Press, London, 2002.

Chang, Ha-Joon, *Globalisation, Economic Development and the Role of the State*, Zed Books, London and New York, 2003.

Chomsky, Noam, *Profit Over People: Neoliberalism and Global Order*, Madhyam Books, New Delhi, 1999.

Dahl, Robert A., *Polyarchy: Participation and Opposition*, Yale University Press, New Haven, 1971.

Dahl, Robert A., *Democracy and its Critics*, Yale University Press, New Haven, 1989.

Dicken, Peter, *Global Shift*, Chapman, London, 1998.

Eatwell, John, *International Financial Liberalization: The Impact on World Development*, Discussion Paper Series, No. 12, UNDP, New York, 1997.

Eichengreen, Barry, *Globalizing Capital: A History of the International Monetary System*, Princeton University Press, New Jersey, 1996.

Falk, Richard, *On Humane Governance: Toward a New Global Politics*, Polity Press, Cambridge, 1995.

Feigenbaum, Harvey, Jeffrey Henig, and Chris Hamnett, *Shrinking the State: The Political Underpinnings of Privatization*, Cambridge University Press, Cambridge, 1999.

Fukuyama, Francis, "The End of History?," *National Interest*, 16, 1989.

Fukuyama, Francis, *The End of History and the Last Man*, Free Press, New York, 1992.

Gilpin, Robert, *Global Political Economy: Understanding The International Economic Order*, Princeton University Press, New Jersey, 2001.

Gray, John, *False Dawn: The Delusions of Global Capitalism*, Granta Books, London, 1999.

Greider, William, *One World, Ready or Not: The Manic Logic of Global Capitalism*, Simon and Schuster, New York, 1997.

Held, David, and Anthony McGrew (eds.), *Governing Globalization: Power, Authority and Global Governance*, Cambridge University Press, Cambridge, 2003.

Helleiner, Eric, *States and the Reemergence of Global Finance*, Cornell University Press, Ithaca and London, 1994.

Herman, Edward S., and Robert W. McChesney, *The Global Media: The New Missionaries of Corporate Capitalism*, Madhyam Books, New Delhi, 1997.

Hertz, Noreena, *The Silent Takeover: Global Capitalism and the Death of Democracy*, Arrow Books, London, 2002.

Hirst, Paul, and Grahame Thompson, *Globalization in Question: The International Economy and the Possibilities of Governance*, Polity Press, Cambridge, 1999.

Holton, Robert J., *Globalization and the Nation-State*, Macmillan Press Ltd., London, 1998.

Kapur, Devesh, and Richard Webb, *Governance-Related Conditionalities of the International Financial Institutions*, UNCTAD, G-24 Discussion Paper Series 6, UNCTAD, New York and Geneva, 2000.

Khan, L.A., *The Extinction of the Nation-State: A World without Borders*, Kluwer Law International, The Hague, 1996.

Legrain, Philippe, *Open World: The Truth About Globalisation*, Abacus,

Great Britain, 2002.

Moran, Theodore H., *Foreign Direct Investment and Development: The New Policy Agenda for Developing Countries and Economies in Transition*, Institute for International Economics, Washington D.C., 1998.

Mosley, Paul, Jane Harrigan, and John Toye (eds.), *Aid and Power: The World Bank and Policy-based Lending*, Routledge, London, 1991.

Nye, J.S., and J. D. Donohue (eds.), *Governance in a Globalizing World*, Brookings Institution, Washington, D.C., 2000.

O'Brien, Robert, Anne Marie Goetz, Jan Aart Scholte, and Marc Williams, *Contesting Global Governance: Multilateral Economic Institutions and Global Social Movements*, Cambridge University Press, Cambridge, 2000.

Ohmae, Kenichi, *The Borderless World*, Harper Collins, New York, 1990.

Ohmae, Kenichi, *The End of the Nation State: The Rise of Regional Economies*, Free Press, New York, 1995.

Pauly, Louis W., *Who Elected the Bankers?*, Cornell University Press, Ithaca and London, New York, 1997.

Petras, James, and Henry Veltmeyer, *Globalization Unmasked: Imperialism in the 21st Century*, Madhyam Books, New Delhi, 2001.

Pinkney, Robert, *Democracy in The Third World*, Lynne Rienner Publishers, Boulder, 2003.

Robinson, William I., *Promoting Polyarchy: Globalization, US Intervention, and Hegemony*, Cambridge University Press, Cambridge, 1996.

Rodrik, Dani, *Has Globalization Gone Too Far?*, Institute for International Economics, Washington, D.C., 1997.

Rugman, Alan, *The End of Globalization*, Random House Business Book, London, 2000.

Sassen, Saskia, *Losing Control?: Sovereignty in an Age of Globalization*, Columbia University Press, New York, 1996.

Kavaljit Singh

Scholte, J. A., *Globalization: A Critical Introduction*, Palgrave, Basingstoke, 2000.

Schumpeter, Joseph A., *Capitalism, Socialism, and Democracy*, Harper and Brother, New York, 1942.

Shutt, Harry, *A New Democracy: Alternatives to a Bankrupt World Order*, Zed Books, London and New York, 2001.

Singh, Kavaljit, *The Globalization of Finance: A Citizen's Guide*, Zed Books, London and New York, 1998.

Singh, Kavaljit, *Taming Global Financial Flows: Challenges and Alternatives in the Era of Financial Globalization*, Zed Books, London and New York, 2000.

Singh, Kavaljit, *Global Corporate Power: Emerging Trends and Issues*, ASED-PIRC Briefing Paper, New Delhi, 2001.

Singh, Kavaljit, *Tax Financial Speculation: The Case for a Securities Transaction Tax in India*, ASED-PIRC Briefing Paper, New Delhi, 2001.

Singh, Kavaljit, *Multilateral Investment Agreement in the WTO: Issues and Illusions*, Policy Paper No. 1, Asia-Pacific Research Network, Manila, 2003.

Sogge, David, *Give and Take: What's the Matter with Foreign Aid?*, Zed Books, London and New York, 2002.

Soros, George, *The Crisis of Global Capitalism: Open Society Endangered*, Little, Brown and Company, London, 1998.

Soros, George, *Open Society: Reforming Global Capitalism*, Little, Brown and Company, London, 2000.

Strange, Susan, *The Retreat of the State: The Diffusion of Power in the World Economy*, Cambridge University Press, Cambridge, 1996.

Strange, Susan, *States and Markets*, Basil Blackwell, New York, 1988.

Tanzi, Vito, *Taxation in an Integrating World*, Brooking Institution, Washington D.C., 1995.

Thomas, Caroline, *Global Governance, Development and Human Security: The Challenge of Poverty and Inequality*, Pluto Press, London, 2000.

UNCTAD, *Bilateral Investment Treaties in the mid-1990s*, United Nations, New York, 1998.

UNCTAD, *From Adjustment to Poverty Reduction: What is New?*, New York and Geneva, 2002.

UNCTAD, *Trade and Development Report 2002*, United Nations, New York and Geneva, 2002.

UNCTAD, *World Investment Report 2002*, United Nations, New York and Geneva, 2002.

`UNCTAD, *Trade and Development Report 2003*, United Nations, New York and Geneva, 2003.

UNCTAD, *World Investment Report 2003*, United Nations, New York and Geneva, 2003.

UNDP, *Human Development Report 2001*, Oxford University Press, New York, 2001.

UNRISD, *Visible Hands: Taking Responsibility for Social Development*, Geneva, 2000.

Weiss, Linda, and John M. Hobson, *States and Economic Development: A Comparative Historical Analysis*, Polity Press, London, 1995.

Weiss, Linda, *The Myth of the Powerless State: Governing the Economy in a Global Era*, Polity Press, Cambridge, 1998.

Woodward, David, *The Next Crisis: Direct and Equity Investment in Developing Countries*, Zed Books, London and New York, 2002.

World Bank, *Globalization, Growth, and Poverty: Building an Inclusive World Economy*, Oxford University Press, New York, 2002.

Index

generation conditionalities 138; governance conditionality 138-39, 142; policy conditionality 155; second-generation conditionalities 106, 138; structural conditionality 138, 140
Congo 106
corruption 34, 46, 105, 119, 150-52
Costa Rica 56
Croatia 110
crony capitalism 109
Cuba 101
Cuban Liberty and Democratic Solidarity Act 69
Czech Republic 41-2
Czechoslovakia 63

Dahl, Robert A. 110
Dai-Ichi Kangyo 38
DaimlerChrysler 86-7
debt crisis 66
decentralization 120-21
delegative democracy 110
delinking 176
Demirguc-Kunt, Asli 33
deregulation 37, 145, 169
Deterritorialization 13
Detragiache, Enrica 33
devaluation 35
dirty money 113
dispute settlement mechanism 57, 63
Doha 56, 84
Doremus, Paul 165
Dresdner Bank 120

Earth Summit 65
East Timor 103
Eastern Europe 107, 114, 140
Eatwell, John 27
efficient markets hypothesis 22
emerging markets 81
Enron 83, 95, 109, 151
Estonia 38, 42, 68

Ethiopia 135, 167
ethnicity 177-78
Ethyl Corporation 73-4
European Central Bank 118
European Union (EU) 24, 37, 43, 46, 55-6, 69, 78-9, 82, 91, 103, 122, 164, 173-74
Exchange Rate Mechanism 33
expropriation 72-4
Exxon Mobil 86

Feigenbaum, Harvey 151, 168
Fiji 102, 106, 131
Fimaco 119
finance capital 16, 112, 158, 171
Financial Services Agreement 79
financiers 51
Fischer, Stanley 22
foreign direct investment (FDI) 24-6, 29, 71, 81, 85-90, 113-14, 164, 176
Foreign Investment Review Agency 67
France 33, 60, 69, 99, 174
Fuji 38

General Agreement on Tariffs and Trade (GATT) 63, 67, 75; Tokyo Round 67; Uruguay Round 63, 67, 75, 79
General Agreement on Trade in Services (GATS) 56, 67, 71, 77-9; GATS-type approach 91
Geneva 124
George Soros 103
Germany 45-6, 63, 90, 166, 174; Bundesbank 44; Landesbanken 46; Mittelstand 46; Sparkassen 46-7
Ghana 25, 81, 110
Global Crossing 109
Global Parliament 126
Global Tax Organization 126
Globality 13

policy ownership 147
polyarchy 110-11
portfolio investments 24, 29, 71, 113-14
Porto Alegre 152
Post-Washington Consensus 137
Poverty Reduction Strategy Papers (PRSPs) 134-35, 139, 147, 149-50
privatization 50, 100, 127, 151, 168
pseudo democracy 110

quantitative restrictions 76

real estate 30
Regulation 57, 95
re-regulation 169
research and development (R&D) 165
restricted democracy 110
Robinson, William I. 111
Rodrik, Dani 27, 168
'rollback' mechanisms 76
Romania 41
Ruggiero, Renato 55
Russia 110, 114, 116, 131, 146, 151
Rwanda 150

Sabirin, Syahril 119
Santiso, Carlos 142, 153
Savings and Loan crisis 32
Scandinavian countries 38
S.D. Myers Inc. 74
Securities and Exchange Commission (SEC) 157
Seko, Mobutu Sese 113, 150
self-fulfilling panics 171
self-fulfilling prophecies 29
Serfin 41
Sharif, Nawaz 107
Shell 113, 169
Sheng, Andrew 43
Sierra Leone 131
Singapore 55, 82

Slovak Republic 41-2, 68
small and medium-sized enterprises (SMEs) 45, 84-5
Smythe, Elizabeth 90
sound economic management 104, 134, 138
South Africa 25, 114, 127
South East Asia 116, 144; countries 33, 109; financial crisis 23, 28, 34, 36, 41, 94, 109, 137, 171
South Korea 28, 36, 41-2, 47, 56, 59, 115, 127
Southern cone countries 33
Spain 43
Special Drawing Rights (SDRs) 155
structural adjustment programs 66, 119, 137
Sub-Saharan Africa 25, 26, 140
Sudan 103
Summers, Lawrence 120
Switzerland 44, 99

Taiwan 25
Takeshita, Noboru 150
Taliban 102, 108
Tanzania 150
technocratic consensus 18, 153
television 125
Thailand 33, 36, 41-2, 127
'third wave' of democratization 110
'top-down' approach 71, 78
Toye, John 142
Toyota Camry 61
trade facilitation 55
Trade-Related Aspects of Intellectual Property Rights (TRIPs) 79, 82
Trade-Related Investment Measures (TRIMs) 66-7, 70, 75-7, 79, 90
trade unions 92, 107, 156
transfer pricing 60, 94, 157
transition economies 44
transnational banks 42
transnational capital 14, 98, 104, 115,